Matters of the Heart

God's Solution for Every Problem

Millie,
I want you to know that
no matte what you are
going through. God does
have a solution for EVERY
matte of the heart.

9/1/2001

Matters of the Heart

God's Solution for
Every Problem

Monifa Robinson Groover

Library of Congress Control Number: 2020924672

Publication Cataloging-in-Publication Data

Matters of the Heart: God's Solution for Every Problem
by Monifa Robinson Groover

198 page cm.

ISBN: 978-0-9836776-7-3 Paperback

978-0-9836776-8-0 ePub

978-0-9836776-9-7 Mobi

Printed in the United States of America

DEDICATION

Matters of the Heart was originally created for a friend in need. But what she didn't know, is the rest of the world needed it too.

ETERNAL DEVOTION

I am eternally grateful to:

God: my Father, my Rock, and my Foundation for giving me the vision. I will forever honor, bless, praise, and magnify your name.

Jesus Christ: the Son, my Savior and Friend. Your faithfulness could never be compared. Thank You. You are my strength. Ultimately, I look to You to help carry me out the work God has set before me.

Holy Spirit: You've been my Teacher, Comforter, Protector, and constant Guide. For this, I am forever devoted and eternally grateful.

TABLE OF CONTENTS

Table of Contents

ACKNOWLEDGEMENTS

Jamie Groover:

> Words cannot adequately express my gratitude toward the Most High for placing you in my life. Thank you for your wonderful gift of love and your loyalty. Thank you for your prayers and support. You are truly a man beyond measure and a husband beyond all comparison. I love you.

Alice Robinson, my mother and friend:

> I am grateful for your love, prayers, and support. You are truly a shining example of what it means to have a heart for God.

Karima Lane, the best sister and friend:

> You can't choose your family, but you can choose your friends. Well, I didn't have to do either with you, because I got the best of both worlds. When God placed us in each other's lives, God wrapped everything into one. I love you.

Tommy Robinson, the best dad a girl could ever ask for:

> You may be gone, but you are never forgotten. You always remain in my heart. I love you, Daddy.

Marti and the Rebel Queen Team:

> Thank you for sharing your insight, wisdom, and talent. You are awesome, and because of you the publishing process has been smooth, positive and energizing.

Family, friends, and loved ones:

> It is refreshing to know that in a world so chaotic, God has divinely placed individuals in my life who have deposited seeds of wisdom and encouragement into me. While there are too many to name, I want to thank all of you for your individual gifts of love and support.

Those who were transparent and vulnerable enough to share their story:

> Unbeknownst to you, my heart is filled with even more compassion. I pray for you by name, asking God to fill you with His love, cover you with His grace, and heal every area of your lives. May He, who has begun a good work in you, perform it until the day of Jesus Christ.

FOREWORD

There are those who will encourage us to follow our hearts, but our hearts can tell us anything and lead us in any direction. And those directions are not necessarily the places where God wants us to go. In Jeremiah 17:9 (NIV), the Word tells us, "The heart is deceitful above all things and beyond cure. Who can understand it?" That alone lets us know that pursuing our hearts isn't necessarily the right thing to do.

Based upon each individual's life experiences, or by what or whom they are influenced, his or her heart can be terribly misguided. A heart can convince a person that they are ugly, worthless, stupid, too short, too tall, too fat, too thin, a disappointment, a failure, a nobody; a heart can lead one to believe that he or she isn't even worth the air they breathe. Suicides happen daily because of what the heart says.

In *Matters of the Heart*, Monifa Robinson Groover gets to the heart of the matter. Between the pages of this devotional lies an exhaustive list of emotions and experiences that are tackled one by one. While these feelings and encounters are common among us, they often go unaddressed and untapped, largely because those who face them choose to do so in secret. But whereas we can mask things from other fallible human beings, nothing is hidden from our Almighty God.

Psalm 44:21 assures us that God knows the secrets of our hearts. Those matters that we tuck away in closets and sweep under carpets are in plain view of our heavenly Father, and I believe He has divinely used the pen of Groover to expose those things that the enemy wants sufferers to keep hidden.

Matters of the Heart is a book that could open the door to genuine and candid conversations among both males and females. It attacks the problems head-on, offers biblically sound directions and solutions, and then extends relatable prayers to help those who may be experiencing what has been discussed.

If this book is not a written tool for you, it is surely one for someone you know. All of us have someone in our lives that needs to address matters of the heart.

-Dr. Kendra Norman Holmes

Pastor, Life Coach,
TV Talk Show Host,
8-Time National Bestselling Author

www.RoyaltyWriter.net

INTRODUCTION

The world is filled with so much pain, chaos, and confusion. If we are not careful, we will succumb to societal pressure and become subject to the world's power. It is only when we give our lives over to Jesus Christ, Son of the One True Living God, that we will experience every good and perfect gift He has to offer. His Word declares, "… No good thing will He withhold from those who walk uprightly" (Psalm 84:11b, NKJV). However, despite our commitment to Christ, we encounter challenges here on earth intent on challenging our faith. These challenges often cause us to grow tired and weary. God wants to remind each and every believer that when these challenges arise, He has already provided a solution that speaks to that particular matter of the heart.

Oftentimes we wonder how we should deal with many of these issues: betrayal, insecurity, anger, loneliness, shame, and more. It is possible to overcome these issues. His Word declares, "Yet in all these things we are more than conquerors through Him who loved us" (Romans 8:37, NKJV). You don't have to stick a bandage on your problems only for the glue to lose its strength and tear off before the wound has healed. There is wholeness and complete healing in Jesus. He has an answer for each and every matter of the heart, an answer that will bring "peace… [that] surpasses all understanding" (Philippians 4:7, NKJV).

In order to position yourself for healing, it is important to remember that sometimes healing comes in ways that defy human logic. But this is what God wants. He wants us to stop relying on ourselves and our logic and rely on His supernatural power so we can experience every good thing He has for us.

We have to learn how to bear our burdens in a way that doesn't burden us. And the only way to do this is to allow Christ to do what He was sent here to do. He was sent to relieve us of the burden of sin and from the cares of this world. All we have to do is accept Him and allow His work to be fulfilled in us. I know I make it sound easier than it feels but I truly believe it when God declares in His word that He has the remedy for all our woes, all our unrest, all our turmoil. He says, "Come to me, all of you who are weary and burdened, and I will give you rest. Take up my yoke and learn from me, because I am lowly and humble in heart, and you will find rest for your souls." (Matthew 11:28-29, CSB). This devotional will show you how to live out this scripture. It will show you what steps you need to take to begin the process of healing in your life.

In order to position ourselves for the breakthrough so many desperately need, there also needs to be a shift in mindset. I tell people often, "When we stop treating God like a resource and start treating Him like *the source*, things will change." God is not a way; He is *the* Way. He is not something that should be accessed when all other means have been exhausted. He should be the foundation and basis upon which all decisions are made.

Just like everything else, there are guidelines we must operate within to receive benefits and rewards. When we operate outside the guide-lines we cannot realistically expect to receive the rewards we crave. This devotional is designed to give you some of the guidelines you need to follow to obtain the peace you desire.

Matters of the Heart is a devotional that reminds us of the power we have to overcome our trials by simply connecting with the One who gave His life so that we could live life more abundantly. As you read this devotional, always take a moment to breathe. I mean this both literally and figura-tively. Take a moment to speak the prayers aloud. Trust me, it makes a difference. Always read this devotional secondary to the Word of God, as there could never be anything that compares to the power of His Word.

My hope and prayer is that this devotional will encourage your heart. Remember, no matter is too great or too small, and God does have a solution for every *matter of the heart.*

ABUSED

"subjected to harmful and improper treatment: having suffered abuse"[1]

---

1   *Merriam-Webster Dictionary*, s.v., "abused," accessed December 16, 2020, https://www.merriam-webster.com/dictionary/abused.

The thing about abuse is it comes in so many different forms. It shows up physically, mentally, emotionally, and financially, just to name a few. While we won't debate which type of abuse is worse, let's just say abuse has a way of causing people to think they are less than what God created them to be. When abuse happens long enough and consistently enough there is a part of that person who begins in some way to believe what the abuser is saying.

Oftentimes people believe if the person who loves them continuously says certain things about them, then those things must be true. Our souls are often fed so much junk—from the world and from other people—that it becomes difficult to believe the truth of God's word. We must consistently feed our souls with the truth of God's word. Part of our souls consist of the mind. We must feed our minds with good things.

Here is one thing to remember: God never reveals a defect for the purpose of tearing down. His end game is always to build up. When He reveals an area that is not in alignment with His will, He then begins to perform the delicate surgery needed to repair the breach. However, abuse is pain caused by human sin. The abuser is usually a hurt, insecure individual with issues that started long before you arrived on the scene.

Don't believe the lies of your abuser. Remember this truth from God's word: "I will praise You, for I am fearfully and wonderfully made; Marvelous are Your works, And that my soul knows very well" (Psalm 139:14, NKJV).

If you are being abused it is important to find someone you can talk to without feeling judged. Yes, you should go to God directly, but God also works through people. Abused individuals often feel trapped, isolated, ashamed, and desperate. You need a way out of your situation, but you also need someone who will listen to you with the love of Christ to provide support throughout your process.

Prayer:

Lord, thank You for being my Protector. I look to You to provide me with the wisdom, guidance, and resources I need. I ask You to restore my faith and confidence in You. Help me to believe that I am fearfully and wonderfully made and that I am not who my abuser says I am. I am who YOU say I am. I am Your treasured possession. I am Your child. I am "more than a conqueror" (Romans 8:37, NKJV). Help me to find comfort in You. I pray with expectation and in alignment with Your will and in Your Son Jesus's name, Amen.

Reflections:

_____

_____

_____

_____

_____

ANGER

"a strong feeling of displeasure and usually of antagonism"[2]

---

2   Ibid., s.v. "anger," accessed, December 16, 2020, https://www.merriam-webster.com/dictionary/anger.

Well, first of all, who hasn't been angry? I mean, maybe there's somebody out there, but the average individual has been angry at least once in their lifetime. Anger can manifest itself in different ways, at different points and times. Some people cry when they get angry. Some people hurt other people when they are angry. Some people hurt themselves.

One thing is for sure: When anger is not dealt with appropriately, it festers. When this happens, bitterness and vindictive spirits now have an open portal into your soul. I'm not talking about simply being frustrated because you are running late for work. I'm talking about anger that can build into resentment, bitterness, and rage.

Here is the thing about anger. Anger is usually an indication of a deeper emotion: hurt, disappointment, pain, or low self-esteem. Anger is really good at detaching you from these feelings and from what's really going on. Think about it, once you really deal with what's really going on—in you and in the situation that angered you—the anger usually subsides. It's almost miraculous how the intensity of the anger will begin to die down.

To deal with the root of anger, we have to be willing to address the emotions lying beneath the surface. These emotions are what we truly fight. When we think about the fruit of the Spirit that Christ offers, we find that He is the source of everything we need to combat the negative emotions threatening to eat us alive (Galatians 5:22-23).

Many of us have heard people say, "It's not the emotion that's bad, but how we deal with it that makes it bad." Well, that is true to a degree. When directed toward anything that is not aligned with the will of God (righteous anger), it is okay. God will give you direction on how to deal with that situation. It is in your humanness where you have the tendency to become emotional and execute unrighteous judgment. If you are not careful, you will become overwhelmed and your thoughts will become caught up in feelings, thus leaving your actions to become impure.

Let's not be fooled. Regardless of how anger manifests itself, once seeds of hurt, disappointment and pain are planted, they can take root and grow into something beyond your control. Before you realize it, you are dealing with a poisonous weed choking your heart, hindering you from sharing the fruit of the Spirit. At that point, it is usually too late.

This is why taking a moment to breathe—both literally and figuratively—is necessary. Make sure to do a self-assessment to ensure you respond to various matters appropriately. Have a little talk with Jesus to have Him guide you in how to deal with unsettling thoughts and feelings.

Prayer:

Lord, help me to identify and deal with the emotions that lie beneath my anger. You are the only One who can truly bring me peace. Help me to develop a closer walk with You so the fruit that comes from your Holy Spirit can manifest itself in my life. I no longer want anger to occupy my heart. Thank You for removing the anger and bringing about a peace that goes beyond my human understanding (Philippians 4:7). I pray with expectation and in alignment with Your will and in Your Son Jesus's name, Amen.

Reflections:

_____

_____

_____

_____

_____

ANXIOUS

"characterized by extreme uneasiness of mind or brooding fear about some contingency"[3]

3   Ibid., s.v. "anxious," accessed December 16, 2020, https://www. merriam-webster.com/dictionary/anxious.

While some people have severe bouts of anxiety that require medical intervention, I believe there is another subset of individuals that experience anxiety simply because of their mindset. Sometimes, when we look at a lot of situations, we feel anxious and nervous, because of what we think is going to happen and from what we've experienced in the past. It all starts in our mind which is why visualization techniques are so powerful.

At the core, you have to change your thinking. When you change your thinking, you change your life. I know it sounds cliché, but it is so true. Even the Bible says, "...be transformed by the renewing of your mind,..." (Romans 12:2b, NKJV). So this is not just a worldly cliché.

When we change our thought process, embrace the truth of God's Word, and rely on Christ to help us, we know He will never lead us astray.

Knowing that He covers us in His blood and gives us protection, guidance, and salvation decreases our anxiety. When a parent has proven themselves to be a good provider, the child is never anxious for food. When the child gets hungry, they may become easily excitable and constantly ask when they are going to eat, but they are never actually worried about whether or not they will eat.

It's the same way with God. When we learn to see God through the eyes of a child, we won't experience as much anxiety as we do. Now, we are not going to act like real life isn't happening. Life has a way of throwing curve balls that present legitimate concerns that often test your faith. This is where you will begin to see how secure your foundation really is.

Take in this truth from Philippians 4:6-7: "Be anxious for nothing, but in everything by prayer and supplication, with thanksgiving, let your requests be made known to God; and the peace of God, which surpasses all understanding, will guard your hearts and minds through Christ Jesus" (NKJV).

I love God's word because His solutions are so simple. Oftentimes we try to figure out how we can make things happen in our own power, but it is "'not by [our] might or [our] power, but by My Spirit,' Says the LORD of hosts" (Zechariah 4:6, NKJV).

So what are you supposed to do when anxiety begins to rear its ugly head in your life? First, take a minute to breathe, both literally and fig-uratively. Then, remind yourself of the grace of God. Remind yourself that nothing has ever caught Him by surprise. No matter how your situation turns out, God has everything in con-trol. Then, simply ask God for guidance on how to proceed.

Prayer:

Lord, thank You for being the Alpha and Omega. Thank You for knowing the end from the beginning. I am so grateful that I have opened my heart to You and allowed You to rule in my life. Because You are all-knowing, I have confidence in You and I trust You. I am at peace knowing that You always have my best interests at heart. Anxiety can no longer reside in me because Your peace lives in my heart. I can walk confidently in Your will knowing that I am protected. I pray in expectation and in alignment with Your will and in Your Son Jesus's name, Amen.

Reflections:

_____

_____

_____

_____

_____

BETRAYED

*"treacherously abandoned,
deserted or mistreated"*[4]

4   Ibid., s.v. "betrayed," accessed December 16, 2020, https://
www.merriam-webster.com/dictionary/betrayed.

Betrayal comes in many forms but most often it manifests itself in relationships. Trust does not come easy for most. When someone violates your trust or confidence, it usually tears at the soul. It's one thing to be betrayed by someone you loved and trusted. But imagine that person using God's name as their justification. Even worse, imagine everyone else knowing about this façade and never telling you, leaving you to discover the truth on your own.

The betrayal hits you harder. Now, the people you thought cared have proven they only cared about themselves. No one cared about you enough to even send you an anonymous note to provide fair warning. Your life never really mattered to them.

Oftentimes, the after-effects of betrayal are shame, guilt, isolation, anger, and depression. These are the emotions you deal with when your dreams and your world seem to shatter. You ask yourself, *How can I move beyond this? How can I ever trust another person again? How can I trust a God who would allow this?*

Then it happens. You stop praying. Attending church is no longer a priority to you. You delete the Bible app from your phone. You stop believing. Just when you think your life couldn't get any worse, it begins to spiral out of control. You now begin to live a reckless life.

But, you say, *I am not using drugs or alcohol, so how is my life reckless?* Anytime you operate outside of the will of God, you endanger yourself and the lives of others because now your thoughts and actions are subject to Satan's rule. You become negligent, thoughtless, and desperate in your ways.

This is what Satan, your enemy, wants. This is why 1 Peter 5:8 says "Be sober, be vigilant; because your adversary the devil walks about like a roaring lion, seeking whom he may devour" (NKJV). When your life becomes reckless, you are now easy prey.

I get it. When you are in pain, this may be a difficult concept to grasp. However, it is declared in His word, "God *is* not a man, that He should lie…" (Numbers 23:19a, NKJV). We must remember that the images we see in others don't always represent Christ. Don't let the bad seeds convince you that there are no good ones out there. You may feel so broken and disheartened by how man has treated you that you could never imagine anyone, not even God being better. I promise there is something supernatural about the healing power of God.

Prayer:

Lord, You know the pain I feel as a result of betrayal and broken trust. I am grateful that I can call out to You in the midst of my pain and You are right there ready to provide comfort. Only You can release my pain and restore my heart.

Thank You for helping me see Your love for what it is: pure and undefiled. Thank You for restoring my faith in You. I pray with expectation and in alignment with Your will and in Your Son Jesus's name, Amen.

Reflections:

_____

_____

_____

_____

_____

CONFUSED

"being perplexed or disconcerted"[5]

---

5   Ibid., s.v. "confused," accessed December 16, 2020, https://www.merriam-webster.com/dictionary/confused.

When you do your best to operate within the will of God, clearly the cares of this world will leave you confused: about life, about your gift, about your calling, even about your very existence. When you are confused, you endanger yourself. You are desperate. You leave yourself open to utilizing any and every option available to you to bring clarity and peace, regardless of its alignment with God's will.

We come into this world with everyone from parents to teachers, preachers and friends telling us what we are supposed to be doing. But when you try doing those things sometimes you find yourself still unfulfilled and unclear about what direction to go. You also find yourself unsure of how to even go about figuring it out. Even when you have a natural ability to do something, you can still find yourself feeling unfulfilled, like you are not doing the "right" thing even if it's what God has called you to do.

When you've been trained to think one way for so long, it's hard to think any other way, even when that other way is the path that unmasks the mystery and moves you closer to clarity. It's difficult to rewire your brain. The only way to position ourselves so we can operate with clarity and not confusion is through seeking His wisdom. Since we know "…God is not *the author* of confusion but of peace," then it would make perfect sense to go to Him for clarity on any and everything regarding our lives (1 Corinthians 14:33a, NKJV).

When you purchase a new piece of technology, and you are confused about how to operate it, you don't often go to the manufacturer for clarity on what to do. We waste so much time and become increasingly frustrated when we go to others or try to figure things out our own. If we would simply start out by going to the manufacturer of our lives—God—you will be given clear instructions on how to move forward.

Another thing that causes confusion is the fact that we, as humans, have the need to know everything and have a plan every step of the way. Don't get caught up in needing to know the end from the beginning. That's God's job. David said in Psalm 119:105, "Your word *is* a lamp to my feet and a light to my path" (NKJV). This means, as long as you seek Him first and walk in His will, He will lead and guide your every step. You may not see the end right now, but He will shed light on your path so you don't stumble. Since we know He has nothing but wonderful things in store for His people, we don't have to worry about what's at the end of the road.

Prayer:

Lord, I am confused. I have no idea what is going on. I have no idea of who I am or where I am going. It is hard to see the road ahead of me. I do know my desire is to please You and I know that if I look to You, You will lead me out of confusion and into clarity. Therefore, I will put my trust in

You. I will not fear, for You are always with me, and You will never leave me to face the perils of this world alone. I pray with expectation and in alignment with Your will and in Your Son Jesus's name, Amen.

Reflections:

_____

_____

_____

_____

_____

DEFEATED

"[feeling] frustration by nullification or by prevention of success"[6]

---

6   Ibid., s.v. "defeated," accessed December 16, 2020, https://www.merriam-webster.com/dictionary/defeated.

Feelings of defeat don't usually come about from one lost battle. Feeling defeated is usually a byproduct of exhaustion from consistently being in the throes of battles where you often find yourself on the losing side. When this happens, your spirit and your will grow extremely tired. You feel weighed down and stuck. You feel like throwing in the towel. You may be saying to yourself, *Lord I have done all I know how to do. I can't do this anymore.*

When you feel defeated, you not only feel like you can't win in your situation; you may begin to wonder why you aren't winning. One reason may be comparison. Are you feeling overwhelmed and overcome because you constantly compare yourself to others? Comparison is your enemy. It will have you feeling either defeated or prideful every time because you will always find someone who appears to have more or less than you. It's a waste of time, as most people are putting up a façade anyway.

Another reason may be because you are trying to do what only God can do. I am not speaking about taking responsibility and doing your part. I am talking about expecting your work in and of itself to magically open doors. When you operate in faith (since "faith without works is dead"), God then sees you trust Him enough to move and operate within His will, and so now He is obligated to keep His word (James 2:26b, NKJV). His Word declares, "We are hard-pressed on every side, yet not crushed; *we are* perplexed, but not in despair; persecuted, but not forsaken; struck down, but not destroyed" (2 Corinthians 4:8-9, NKJV). And His Word promises "...in all these things we are more than conquerors through Him who loved us" (Romans 8:37, NKJV).

Don't you see? You are *not* defeated, because God is the One fighting your battles for you.

I get it. Sometimes you may feel defeated because you constantly compare yourself to the Word of God and you feel you don't measure up. This is exactly why we need Christ. We need him because in and of ourselves we don't measure up. It is the gift of God (Jesus Christ) and His Holy Spirit that cleanses us so we can measure up. When we truly see that our identity is rooted in Him, we have access to the benefits that come along with being His child. And those benefits include being victorious over the enemy.

Prayer:

Heavenly Father, I am mentally, emotionally, spiritually, and physically tired. I am doing my best, but I feel like I just can't win. I feel defeated. Despite my feelings, I am reminded that I must put my trust and hope in You. You are my defender. You will defeat my enemy. My situation is not hopeless because of You. I pray with expectation and in alignment with Your will and in Your Son Jesus's name, Amen.

Reflections:

_____

_____

_____

_____

_____

DEPRESSED

"low in spirits: sad; especially:
affected by psychological depression"[7]

7   Ibid., s.v. "depressed," accessed December 16, 2020, https://
www.merriam-webster.com/dictionary/depressed.

While there are many people who legitimately suffer from clinical depression, I believe there are far more people who suffer from depression as a result of their human expectations and their disconnectedness from God.

We come into this world with hopes and dreams. We go to school and work hard to become *the best,* and when our hope finally meets our reality, disappointment sets in. When we don't get the job, when the engagement is called off, when the marriage doesn't work out, when we can't lose the weight, it seems that our hopes and dreams are shattered. When this happens one too many times, disappointment begins to shift to sadness and sadness shifts to depression.

Sometimes depression sets in because we are dealing with the consequences of some of our choices and bad decisions. Depression can cause a host of emotional, physical, and psychological concerns to surface. I've been there. I have been stressed and depressed to the point where medical issues became evident. When I went to the doctor, they could not find any medical reason for why I had become sick. The cause was stress and depression, something lab results could not detect. The wonderful thing about God, however, is that He is a healer. He has a remedy for every problem. He wants us to come to Him for everything. He gives clear instructions on combating depression. Psalm 55:22 says, "Cast your burden on the LORD, and he will sustain you; he will never allow the righteous to be shaken" (CSB).

I knew a young lady who was small in her physical stature, but that didn't stop her from saving lives as a firefighter. I asked her one day how she was able to carry 250-pound men out of burning buildings. She laughed. "I get that question all the time," she said. "People focus on the weight. I tell them, it's not just about the weight. It's how you carry the weight that makes a difference." In other words, she could have a 250-pound man that actually feels like he weighs 215 pounds when she's carrying him out the building, simply because she learned methods to carry weight in a way so that it does not feel as heavy as it is.

Life is full of things that weigh us down mentally, emotionally, physically, and spiritually. But the key is to not focus on the weight. The key is learning how to carry the weight so that it does not feel as heavy as it actually is.

Now I'm not saying sadness is not going to hit. I'm not saying depression might not try to rear its ugly head. But I am saying that the blood of Jesus is more powerful than depression. Many times, the reason you spiral downward is because you either didn't plug into the Source from the beginning or you lost connection somewhere along the way.

I am all for doing tangible things"—like taking vacations, being more intentional about our health and wellness, breathing deeply, getting a massage, etc.—to manage stress more effectively. There is nothing wrong with those things, and they are all helpful. However, if we want to truly release the weight of depression, we must plug into God. You must connect yourself to The One who is able to deliver you. I believe that the healing from depression begins once you receive and accept Christ into your life.

Prayer:

Heavenly Father, life has become such a struggle, and my faith in You is being seriously challenged. I come to You today to ask for help. Please strengthen my heart. Help me focus on You every time depression tries to overwhelm me. You tell me in your word, "Come to me, all you who are weary and burdened, and I will give you rest" (Matthew 11:28, NIV). So I come to You knowing that Your word is true. I pray with expectation and in alignment with Your will and in Your son Jesus's name, Amen.

Reflections:

_____

_____

_____

_____

_____

DEVASTATED

"brought to a state of ruin or destruction"[8]

---

8   Ibid., s.v. "devastated," accessed December 16, 2020, https://
www.merriam-webster.com/dictionary/devastated.

There are so many things that happen in life that can devastate you. Things like the death of a loved one or an unfavorable diagnosis from the doctor can throw you for a loop. When these situations hit, many people ask God the famous question: why? There is nothing wrong with seeking God for understanding about why things happen, but even with our curious minds, we must remember God's sovereignty.

In your devastation you may say, *Lord, I'm following Your Word and I'm doing Your will. Why did You allow this to happen?* Sometimes in your devastation you may feel God's delay was the issue. Rest assured that God has a reason and He is never late.

One of the hardest but best things to remember sometimes when you are hit with devastating news is that nothing catches God by surprise. No matter how out of control things may appear, they are always in His control because nothing happens without His permission. When we remember God's sovereignty and look to Him, we gain a little clarity that will allow us to see past the pain. Part of that clarity comes from knowing that you will not have all the answers, but you are connected to the One who does.

Think of it this way. When you get on a plane, you don't know how to fly the plane, but you trust the pilot enough to have a seat and let him do his job. God wants us to trust Him just like you would that pilot. He wants us to know that despite any turbulence we may experience He will get us to our destination. He will protect us along the way. Whatever life blows our way, "He heals the brokenhearted and bandages their wounds" (Psalm 147:3, CSB). When you feel emotionally shattered and distraught, remember that there is no devastation too great for God. He can transform and heal your heart, and His blood can restore you.

How does He heal your broken heart and bandage Your wounds? He may do it by giving you rest and comfort when you read His word and when you pray. He may speak a word to you while you sleep or send some comforting words through someone. He always gives hope to His people. His ways are beyond us, and they work.

Prayer:

Lord, thank You for showing me that nothing happens without your permission. You are never surprised or caught off guard by my circumstances. Help me to remember that I can still be at peace even when devastation threatens to bring me down, because my hope is in You. You are sovereign and I know the plans You have for me are designed to give me hope and a future (Jeremiah 29:11, CSB). I pray with expectation and in alignment with Your will and in Your Son Jesus's name, Amen.

Reflections:

_____

_____

_____

_____

_____

DISAPPOINTED

"defeated in expectation or hope"[9]

---

9 Ibid., s.v. "disappointed," accessed December 16, 2020, https://www.merriam-webster.com/dictionary/disappointed.

Many times, we feel let down when our expectations are not met. When things happen the way you want them to, it feels like they're going well. But when things are not operating in your favor, that is usually when disappointment surfaces.

Of course, it is human to feel disappointed when something doesn't turn out the way you want it to. But the key is to quickly remind yourself that everything is going to be okay. God has a plan. I know you wish He would let you in on the details. Sometimes He does, and sometimes He doesn't. But rest assured, whether you know every detail or not, you know one thing for sure: He tells you "'...I know the plans I have for you,' declares the Lord, 'plans to prosper you and not to harm you, plans to give you hope and a future'" (Jeremiah 29:11, NIV).

Think back to all the times you were disappointed about something, only to feel grateful later on when some things were revealed to you. Think about how God saved your life and you didn't know it at the time. Or what about the time you thought you wanted a certain job only to find out the company folded soon after you were told "no?" Or what about the time you felt embarrassed that the wedding was called off only to find out you dodged a bullet?

I know you may be saying to yourself, *That's why I don't trust anybody but myself.* Well, my dear, the

Word even speaks to that. Proverbs 28:26 says, "The one who trusts in himself is a fool, but one who walks in wisdom will be safe" (CSB). You can't even trust yourself. Haven't you let your own self down before? This is why we have to walk in the wisdom of God.

It would be foolish of me to tell you never to feel disappointed. After all, we live in a world where disappointment is inevitable. But I will say, one way to deal with the pain of disappointment is to remember to place your trust and hope in the One who will never let you down, the One who has plans to prosper you and give you a future. And guess what: He controls the future, too. He will never disappoint His children because He always keeps His word. It doesn't get any better than that.

Prayer:

Heavenly Father, I come before You with a heavy heart. Life hasn't turned out like I expected. I feel disappointed and let-down. Help me to have an eternal perspective. Help me to use my experiences as opportunities to draw closer to You. Please shape me more and more into the image of your Son. I pray with expectation and in alignment with Your will and in Your Son Jesus's name, Amen.

Reflections:

_____

_____

_____

_____

_____

DISTRUSTFUL

"having or showing skepticism"[10]

---

10 Ibid., s.v. "distrustful," accessed December 16, 2020, https://www.merriam-webster.com/dictionary/distrustful.

There are so many reasons you may be suspicious, apprehensive or lack faith. Life is not easy, and it has a way of creating doubt and embedding distrust in your heart if you are not careful. You must be self-aware. Oftentimes, people enter into a situation where, because of their previous experiences, they automatically distrust people and things. There's always a red flag raised.

Some have an attitude of, "I trust you until you give me a reason not to." On the other hand, some believe you're guilty until proven innocent. Either way, often the things we experience in life cause us to be skeptical and untrusting of others.

This is where faith comes in. We have to remember this is a spiritual walk. God operates from a spiritual perspective, so we cannot try to implement human logic into the equation and expect things to work out God's way. The Bible says, "Trust in the Lord with all your heart, and do not rely on your own understanding..." (Proverbs 3:5, CSB).

There is something about relying on God that brings peace and comfort. If you are scared, I encourage you to simply test the waters. God will always keep His promise. His track record is perfect. Unlike man, God is dependable. You will find that He is the only one you can ever really trust.

Prayer:

Heavenly Father, I have been so hurt and betrayed by others. I bring You my pain and I ask You to mend my broken heart. I do not want to allow my experiences to blind me and keep me from putting my trust in You. You are the only one who has ever been consistent and true. I trust that You will always lead and guide me into all truth. Help me to remember that, despite my experience, there is still hope in You. I pray in expectation and in alignment with Your will and in Your Son Jesus's name, Amen.

Reflections:

_____

_____

_____

_____

_____

FEAR

"an unpleasant emotion caused by
anticipation or awareness of danger"[11]

---

11 Ibid., s.v. "fear," accessed December 16, 2020, https://www.merriam-webster.com/dictionary/fear.

Fear is a battle fought primarily in the mind. The mind is more powerful than we know. There is a reason why 1 Peter 1:13 says, "Therefore, with your minds ready for action, be sober-minded and set your hope completely on the grace to be brought to you at the revelation of Jesus Christ" (CSB). You need a sound mind to make sound judgments to fight your battles. Your mind must be ready for action before anything else.

If you don't have a sound mind, rooted and grounded in the Word of God, fear will take you down a rabbit hole, unable to think clearly and scrambling for solutions. Fear never allows you to operate confidently from a place of purpose. Fear only allows you to operate from emotion. We all know that operating from emotion leads to erratic decisions.

The enemy uses intimidation as a weapon to instill fear. Remember, "God has not given us the spirit of fear..." (2 Timothy 1:7a, NKJV). Now, let's be sensible. If there is a lion running after you, of course fear comes over you and you run for safety. But when God says He has not given us the spirit of fear, He is talking about the fact that He has not given us the spirit that keeps us from moving confidently in His will, doing the work He has called us to do. He's given us the spirit of "power and of love and of a sound mind" (2 Timothy 1:7b, NKJV). God has given us Himself, and you can't get more confident than that.

Fear has a double personality. It can show up fierce one minute and laid-back the next. Sometimes the fear is overwhelming and sometimes it creeps up on you. One minute, you are confident in God and the next minute, you aren't. We always need to keep our eyes on Jesus. We cannot give the enemy any room in our lives. This is why we must keep our minds on God at all times. He promises to keep us in perfect peace if we keep our minds stayed on Him (Isaiah 26:3, NKJV). Remember how Peter walked on water until he took his eyes off Jesus. Remember: fear is never greater than the blood of Jesus Christ.

You must be rooted and grounded in God's Word so you can have the confidence to carry out His will in every area of life. We should be able to walk with boldness and say, "I can do all things through Christ who strengthens me" (Philippians 4:13, NKJV).

The enemy will continue to do his job. The question is, will you do your job as a believer in Jesus Christ and stay rooted in His Word? Will you fight the enemy every time he tries to instill fear in your heart?

Prayer:

Lord, as You know, I am struggling with fear. I ask that You release me from it. Every time fear tries to rear its ugly head, remind me of Your Word. Help me to walk confidently in Your will.

I know that if I trust and follow Your plan, I am more than a conqueror and will be triumphant in tearing down the enemy's tactics of intimidation under Your covering grace. I pray with expectation and in alignment with Your will and in Your Son Jesus's name, Amen.

Reflections:

_____

_____

_____

_____

_____

FORGOTTEN

"to [be] treat[ed] with inattention or disregard"[12]

---

12 Ibid., s.v. "forgotten," accessed December 16, 2020, https://www.merriam-webster.com/dictionary/forgotten.

At the core, everybody wants to be loved, valued, and respected. When this happens, you feel great. But when these things are missing, you feel unimportant, pushed to the side, unvalued, and eventually forgotten. This is a lonely place to be. The busyness of life will have you feel like others have forgotten you. It's not that they don't love you, but you come to the realization that you are not high on their list of priorities. You may feel forgotten by family, friends, and loved ones. There may have been times where you felt as though God had forgotten you. You may feel like God is not answering your prayers. You may feel like He is not sending you comfort or peace in your loneliness, but is instead leaving you out on your own.

The truth of the matter is the facts don't always reflect the truth. Sounds crazy, right? Let me explain. Jesus says "...I am the way, the truth, and the life..." (John 14:6a, CSB). When we look at facts, we are looking at things with our natural eyes. The fact might be that you lost your job and your bank account balance is close to zero. But as a child of God you can rest in the *truth* that "... my God will supply all your needs according to his riches in glory in Christ Jesus" (Philippians 4:19, CSB). The truth is, "...I have not seen the righteous abandoned or his children begging for bread" (Psalm 37:25b, CSB).

The enemy will capitalize on your feelings. He will make you feel like what you see is the end of the story. But God says this is not so. When you see God's hand in your situation, you see an entirely different story. If your perspective is predicated on your view of the world, you will always feel lost and forgotten. But if your perspective is predicated on your view of God, you will always feel love and hope.

Always remember: God has not forgotten you. I firmly believe that, even in the middle of the most turbulent storm, He always has a way of reminding His children that they are loved, protected, and remembered. We just have to remain obedient and connected to Him. If a natural parent never forgets their children, what makes you think God will forget His? Just because you don't feel His presence does not mean you are forgotten. You are more precious to Him than you will ever know.

Prayer:

Heavenly Father, I admit I have become distracted and fixated on my problems instead of You. This has caused me to feel as if you have forgotten me and left me all alone. Please forgive me for doubting Your Word. I believe You when You say You will never leave me or forsake me, and that You would keep me in perfect peace if I stay focused on You (Deuteronomy 31:6c, NKJV; Isaiah 26:3, NKJV). I pray with expectation and in alignment with Your will and in Your Son Jesus's name, Amen.

Reflections:

_____

_____

_____

_____

_____

GUILT

"a feeling of deserving blame for offenses"[13]

13 Ibid., s.v. "guilt," accessed December 16, 2020, https://www.merriam-webster.com/dictionary/guilt.

To me, feeling guilty is defined as feeling as though you're to blame for something; feeling an overwhelming sense of responsibility for violating, oppressing, or causing harm to a person directly or indirectly. You may also feel like you have gone against your moral compass, feeling an overwhelming sense of remorse for an offense or wrongdoing that you've done. Oftentimes, when you feel guilty, there's a deep sense of pain and anguish that lives within. If it's not dealt with swiftly and appropriately, it can lead to depression, isolation, and regret. If you are not careful, you can wallow in it for too long, pulling you into a pit that's too hard to climb out of.

Guilt oftentimes is associated with a feeling of failure, and who ever wants to fail? Failure is not a good feeling. But God has a remedy for that, too. Even David said, "My flesh and my heart may fail, but God is the strength of my heart and my portion forever" (Psalm 72:26, NKJV).

The only way for God to be your strength is if you allow Him to be the head of your life. He must take first place. When you don't put God first, feelings of failure and guilt will overwhelm you. The emotions will become too massive to deal with on your own. With these emotions, depression, isolation, and suicidal thoughts are not far behind. This is where the enemy wants you. He wants you to fall into this pit of guilt and shame. He does not want you to know the redemptive power of Christ's love. Christ, however, wants us to come to repentance of our wrongdoing, change our mindset, and do the right thing. Christ came to redeem us and free us from our wrongdoing. He didn't come to condemn us; He came to save us (John 3:17, NKJV). When He died on the cross and rose from the grave, He freed all believers from guilt and shame. He tells us in His Word, "There is therefore now no condemnation to those who are in Christ Jesus, who do not walk according to the flesh, but according to the Spirit" (Romans 8:1, NKJV). Don't fall prey to the enemy's tactics. Christ is waiting to free you today.

Prayer:

Heavenly Father, please forgive me for my wrongdoing and release me from my guilt. I open my heart to You, Lord. I want to experience the redemptive power of Your love. There is no failure in You. Thank You for being a light in darkness. I pray with expectation and in alignment with Your will and in Your Son Jesus's name, Amen.

Reflections:

_____

_____

_____

_____

_____

HOPELESS

"having no expectation of good or success"[14]

14 Ibid., s.v. "hopeless," accessed December 16, 2020, https://www.merriam-webster.com/dictionary/hopeless.

When you feel hopeless, you feel as though there is no remedy or cure. You only see things through the eyes of despair. As a result, you make decisions based on the (supposed) fact that things will never work out.

One reason people lose hope so easily is because they have continuously placed their hope in someone or something unsure. When you are so often disappointed, it is easy to feel like nothing good is going to come. Is your hope in your job? Your spouse? Your bank account? Your education? Is your happiness predicated on these things? If these things fail, would you feel all hope is gone? The remedy for hopelessness is to ask ourselves, *Where are we placing our hope?* Do we have great expectations in this fleeting world that is passing away before our very eyes, or do we place our hope in Jesus Christ, who never fails?

God tells us in Jeremiah 29:11, "'For I know the plans I have for you'—this is the LORD's declaration—'plans for your well-being, not for disaster, to give you a future and a hope'" (CSB). The reason God can make this declaration is because His word is sure. Everything He speaks comes to pass. No other person can make the same claim.

God is a restorer. He can mend your brokenness and bring you into the light out of the darkness of your situation. His supernatural power can make you believe again. All you have to do is be open to receiving His love and following Him. If we place our expectation in Christ, we will never be disappointed.

Prayer:

Heavenly Father, I admit I have wrongly placed my hope in people and things. I ask for Your forgiveness. I now know I need to place my hope in You and You alone. Please deliver me and restore my hope. I put my trust in You. I praise You and know You are faithful to deliver. I pray with expectation and in alignment with Your will and in Your Son Jesus's name, Amen.

Reflections:

_____

_____

_____

_____

_____

IMPATIENT

"…restless or short of temper especially under irritation, delay, or opposition"[15]

---

15 Ibid., s.v., "impatient," accessed December 16, 2020, https://www.merriam-webster.com/dictionary/impatient.

So often we look at others as they enjoy their blessings and wonder, *When will I receive my blessing? When will my change come? When will I be able to experience the fruits of my labor?* Well, the answer is simple: it will happen when it's your time. You must understand that time is relative and, more often than not, your schedule and timeline are often inaccurate. Does this mean you shouldn't plan and set goals? Of course not. However, you do not need to follow and set your sights on goals that others have. You need to be in tune with the Holy Spirit, first and foremost. The Holy Spirit will provide guidance and will inform you of the pace you need to keep. When you do this, you will then be able to say with assurance, "My time will come."

How do I deal with impatience effectively? you ask. Well, patience and faith work hand in hand. Every moment in time is filled with purpose. When you recognize this, you can rest assured knowing that all things work together for your good and for His glory (Romans 8:28, CSB). However, waiting with patience does not imply that action stops. It simply means you have an awareness and a confidence that God has your best interests at heart. You see, while you are doing your part, all you can do is ultimately rely on God to accomplish what no man can. You cannot endure any situation with calmness if you do not hope and believe that regardless of how things look, everything will ultimately work out.

Patience also builds character. Never underestimate the strength and power embedded in the process. Most people hate the process because they want to get painlessly from point A to point Z. I get it. The process is rarely pleasant and often painful. It takes you out of your comfort zone and places you in situations that stretch you. God has a step-by-step plan for how to go through the process with patience. He tells us in Romans 12:12, "Rejoice in hope; be patient in affliction; be persistent in prayer" (CSB).

I know this is easier said than done. But remember: consistency is key. The Word of God never disappoints. I know first-hand if I focus and obsess over the process, I will most likely end up miserable. However, if I stay focused on God's Word, I remain encouraged to keep pushing forward.

Prayer:

Heavenly Father, when life seems uncertain and presents disappointment, or my plans get interrupted, teach me to handle it with grace. Remind me to focus on You and Your Word. Help me to respond with love, wisdom, and patience, and to trust Your timing. I know that when I follow You, all things are working for my good and Your glory. I pray with expectation and in alignment with Your will and in Your son Jesus's name, Amen.

Reflections:

_____

_____

_____

_____

_____

INDECISIVE

"marked by or prone to indecision; irresolute"[16]

---

16 Ibid., s.v. "indecisive," accessed December 16, 2020, https://www.merriam-webster.com/dictionary/indecisive.

We live in a world full of options. We have a lot of decisions to make and we can become very indecisive, not knowing which way to turn, what to do, or even who to speak to. This can be very overwhelming.

Before making decisions, we must become still, seek God, and listen and follow His command. I know this can be challenging. Sometimes God responds right away and sometimes it seems like He is in the control tower keeping our plane in a holding pattern. Sometimes He gives us answers that make us happy, and sometimes He gives answers that make you raise an eyebrow and wonder if you heard Him correctly. Regardless of God's response, seeking Him in all things and doing what He says remain your only options if you want to ensure a positive outcome.

Sometimes you may be fearful of making the wrong move. Rest assured, even when you do not know what to do in the waiting, if you make a move that was not the best to make, He will keep you and protect you. But the key is to always ensure that your heart, mind, and intentions line up with the Word of God. He has your best interests at heart, and He will show you the way. He loves His children, so He will close doors that need to be closed and open doors that need to be opened.

Remember, waiting on God is not about sitting down and twiddling your thumbs, expecting everything to fall into your lap. It's about intertwining God into every facet of your life and serving Him in the ways He directs you.

Jeremiah 33:3 says, "'Call to Me, and I will answer you, and show you great and mighty things, which you do not know.'" (NKJV). If we want guidance and wisdom, God wants us to seek it from Him. One thing I love about God is that He provides wisdom and guidance in so many ways. It may be a still small voice, a dream, a scripture, a sermon, or even through a one-on-one conversation with another believer in Christ. Keep your eyes and ears open for His direction as you go forth in your decisions.

Prayer:

Heavenly Father, I have made decisions in the past without consulting You. These decisions have left me hurt and broken-hearted. Please forgive me. I am now committed to seeking You first in all things. I know that if I seek Your guidance and wisdom You will never lead me astray. Lord, help me to follow Your direction. I pray with expectation and in alignment with Your will and in Your Son Jesus's name, Amen.

Reflections:

INSECURITY

"deficient in assurance:
beset by fear and anxiety"[17]

17 Ibid., s.v. "insecurity," accessed December 16, 2020, https://
www.merriam-webster.com/dictionary/insecurity.

Feelings of rejection often lead to insecurity. When you keep applying for jobs and no one wants to hire you. When you try to make friends and it seems like no one wants to talk to you. When your spouse no longer wants to be married to you. When your parents tell you "no." The list goes on and on. It is easy to lose confidence or feel inadequate and unsure of yourself when you feel rejected.

The Bible never talks about being secure and having confidence in yourself. I am not saying you should not want to feel good about yourself. I am saying the one true boost to your self-esteem and self-worth is to know who you are in Christ Jesus. Your security should never lie in your network, in your job, in your spouse, or in your money. All those things are temporary and will eventually fail. Your security should lie in God. Confidence is the reliance on something or someone. But to truly walk in confidence, you have to walk in Christ. When the Apostle Paul said, "I can do all things through Christ who strengthens me," he was clear about who he put his trust in (Philippians 4:13, NKJV). He knew the only reason he could do anything was because of Christ.

God's solution for insecurity is to remember that it's not you but the power of God inside of you that gives you unfailing strength. If you rely on God's power and follow His lead, you will never need to be insecure, because you know you win in the end.

Prayer:

Heavenly Father, help me break free from the chains of insecurity. Sometimes I question who I am and my self-worth. Forgive me for not acknowledging Your power. Cancel the damaging effect from years of rejection, abuse, and negative self-talk. Help me see that I am fearfully and wonderfully made (Psalm 139:14a, NKJV). I pray with expectation and in alignment with Your will and in Your Son Jesus's name, Amen.

Reflections:

_____

_____

_____

_____

_____

ISOLATED

"…alone…"[18]

18 Ibid., s.v. "isolated," accessed December 16, 2020, https://www.merriam-webster.com/dictionary/isolated.

Sometimes when you feel let down, you may find yourself feeling alone. Have you ever felt like God let you down? If not, great! But I know I've had a few experiences in my life where I felt like God was nowhere around and I was left to fend for myself. Thankfully, I have matured in my relationship with Christ, and I now know that was never the case. But in those moments, I felt alone and far removed from everything I was so sure of.

Feelings of loneliness and rejection will cause you to feel isolated. You can be isolated and still be among a crowd of people. You may also find yourself withdrawing and physically removing yourself from the company of others. God never intended for us to be alone—physically, emotionally, or spiritually—while on this earth. This is why He speaks so much about fellowship and community. He says in 1 John 1:7a, "If we walk in the light as he himself is in the light, we have fellowship with one another..." (CSB). There is strength and power when we can connect and with our Heavenly Father and a community of believers.

When we isolate ourselves, the enemy has a greater opportunity to work on our minds to get us to turn our attention away from God and His redeeming power. But Christ fills the void of loneliness, and He guides us on what to do when the world weighs heavily on us. Through Him, we can combat these feelings of isolation and delight in His presence.

Prayer:

Heavenly Father, sometimes I feel so alone in this world. I feel like no one cares about me or understands me. But Your Word reminds me that you have never forgotten about me. Your Word reminds me that You are always near. Thank You for Your comfort. I pray with expectation and in alignment with Your will and in Your Son Jesus's name, Amen.

Reflections:

_____

_____

_____

_____

_____

JEALOUSY

"a jealous disposition, attitude, or feeling"[19]

19 Ibid., s.v. "jealousy," accessed December 16, 2020, https://www.merriam-webster.com/dictionary/jealousy.

When you are jealous, you have a sense of entitlement. What causes a person to feel they deserve more than others? Some might describe entitlement as "an unrealistic, unmerited, or inappropriate expectation of favorable living conditions and favorable treatment at the hands of others."[20]

The bottom line is this: Jealousy leads you to have an inflated sense of yourself. We are cautioned about this in Romans 12:3b, "...not to think of himself more highly than he should think. Instead, think sensibly..." (CSB). We are warned of the dangers when we do not follow this Word. The danger is jealousy. Along with jealousy comes anger, lies, deception, selfishness, hate, resentment, bitterness, and hostility. Don't be deceived. You may be saying to yourself, *This is overkill. I don't* hate *so and so. I just wish I had what they had.* Well, when you ruminate on any thought long enough, your senses and desires become heightened on that thing. You will soon find yourself pulled into doing whatever is necessary to fulfill those thoughts and desires.

Jealousy will also cause you to become ungrateful and depressed. You will find yourself unsatisfied and unappreciative of the things you have.

---

20 "Sense of Entitlement," Out of the FOG, accessed December 7, 2020, https://outofthefog.website/top-100-trait-blog/2015/11/4/sense-of-entitlement, quoted in Robert Porter, "The Psychology Behind Sense of Entitlement," Better Help, last modified June 25, 2020.

Comparing yourself to others is one sure way to find yourself headed down this path. Oftentimes, we are only privy to seeing other people's glory without knowing or experiencing the depths of their story. If we truly understood the amount of pain someone may have endured, we would be joyful for them when we see blessings manifest in their lives. You would also take comfort in knowing that the God you serve is able to bless you and "do exceeding abundantly above all [you can] ask or think, according to the power that worketh in us." (Ephesians 3:20, KJV). There is no power greater than the power of the Holy Spirit.

Jealousy is a heart issue and we must go to the spiritual cardiologist to get this matter resolved. Christ is the best cardiologist ever. When He performs heart surgery, you are guaranteed to see results. Your outlook will change, and you will see jealousy fade away.

Prayer:

Heavenly Father, I have found myself feeling jealous and coveting what others have. God, please remove these ungodly feelings from my heart. Transform me so I may feel love, joy, and happiness when others are being blessed. Purify my mind from ungodly thoughts and help me to walk in the way that is pleasing to You. I pray with expectation and in alignment with Your will and in Your Son Jesus's name, Amen.

Reflections:

_____

_____

_____

_____

_____

JUDGMENTAL

*"characterized by a tendency to
critique harshly"*[21]

---

21 *Merriam-Webster Dictionary*, s.v. "judgmental," accessed December 16, 2020, https://www.merriam-webster.com/dictionary/judgmental.

This subject usually causes some controversy. You have many that say only God can judge. Well, let's dig into what God says about judging. At the core, judging simply means to conclude something. We judge (or come to conclusions) every day. You decide to wear shorts or long pants depending on the weather. You decide which way to drive home based on the traffic report. Coming to conclusions and decisions based on different variables in and of itself is not bad.

However, when we speak of someone being judgmental, it usually describes someone who often rushes to judgment without reason. This is the type of judgment we want to avoid. As humans, our flesh is easily offended, and with the flesh being the sinful nature of man, you may be offended even when someone is correcting you about something you are doing wrong. Just as we can be easily offended in our flesh, we can also easily offend and cause harm and pain when we judge out of our emotions.

Unlike man, God's judgment is always meant to correct and uplift. When you judge from your flesh, rarely is that critique accompanied by love, compassion, and a desire to see someone grow. It is usually accompanied by anger, self-righteousness, and feelings of superiority. Rarely does it come from a place of wanting to lift someone up and see the other person change their ways. John 7:24b says, "...judge with righteous judgment" (NKJV). When we exercise righteous judgment, we operate like Christ, providing correction with compassion and instruction on how that person can move from their wrongdoing. Righteous judgement aligns itself with the virtues and laws of God. It does not throw scripture at others to make them feel bad. To enact righteous judgment, you must first be righteous. Not self-righteous, but righteous in God's eyes, ensuring that you are aligned with God's Word. Remember: it is God's job to work on the other person's heart, not yours.

Prayer:

Heavenly Father, help me to live holy and righteous before You. When I see others going the wrong way, help me to address the matter with love and compassion, always ready to uplift someone in their time of need. I never want my personal opinion or my emotions to be the basis for judging a matter. I always want to operate in Your will, knowing that your goal is always to restore man back to You. I pray with expectation and in alignment with Your will and in Your Son Jesus's name, Amen.

Reflections:

_____

_____

_____

_____

_____

LONELINESS

"...cut off from others..."[22]

---

22 Ibid., s.v. "loneliness," accessed December 16, 2020, https://www.merriam-webster.com/dictionary/loneliness.

Loneliness causes people to feel empty, alone, and unwanted. Loneliness is more about the internal disconnection from others than it is about the number of people you are physically around, which is why you can be physically surrounded by people and still feel lonely. So the question becomes, *how do you move from feeling lonely and disconnected to connected?*

We have to remember that the Spirit of God is designed to help you deal with this matter of the heart. The Holy Spirit is a comforter. Only He can fill your void. He encourages you to "cast all your cares on him, because he cares about you" (1 Peter 5:7, CSB). This includes going to Him and telling Him you are lonely. When you place your hope in Jesus, there is something that supernaturally happens to lift that burden.

You may be a very practical person and you need to see how God works in concrete, logical detail. So, it may be difficult to see how reading your Bible and talking to an invisible God will make you feel less lonely. But there's something super-natural about the Holy Spirit's power. I can't fully explain how He comforts us, but I guarantee He does. When we do what His Word says, He will pour out His blessing on you.

Well, what does His Word say? The Lord says "Finally, brethren, whatever things are true, whatever things *are* noble, whatever things *are* just, whatever things *are* pure, whatever things *are* lovely, whatever things *are* of good report, if *there is* any virtue and if *there is* anything praiseworthy—meditate on these things" (Philippians 4:8, NKJV). It's hard to feel any negative emotions when you meditate on these things. Joy and comfort have no choice but to overwhelm you and bathe you in their light.

Prayer:

Heavenly Father, I feel so lonely right now. Remind me that You will never leave me or forsake me and that You will always be here with me (Deuteronomy 31:6c, NKJV). I believe Your Word is true. Please send Your Comfort to take away this loneliness. Fill me with peace that surpasses all understanding (Philippians 4:6-7, NKJV). Help me to remember that I am never alone because you are with me (Psalm 23:4c, NKJV). Even when I have no one to talk to, I know I can always talk to You. I pray with expectation and in alignment with Your will and in Your Son Jesus's name, Amen.

Reflections:

_____

_____

_____

_____

_____

LUST

"usually intense or unbridled sexual desire; an intense longing"[23]

23 Ibid., s.v. "lust," accessed December 16, 2020, https://www.merriam-webster.com/dictionary/lust.

Most people only think of lust when they think of strong sexual desire. But you can lust after more than sex. You can lust after things like food, drink, money, fame, power, and knowledge. Lust is a deep, coveting, craving desire, or deep sense of wanting. Lust is focused on pleasing yourself, essentially linked to selfishness and greed. Both greed and selfishness will get you in a whole lot of trouble.

The Word of God is very clear about lust. It says, "For everything in the world—the lust of the flesh, the lust of the eyes, and the pride in one's possessions—is not from the Father, but is from the world" (1 John 2:16, CSB). Your strong desire and attachment to temporary and ungodly things separates you from the love of God.

This world is an illusion. It gives the false impression that love, joy, and peace can be found in accumulating stuff. Lust has an insatiable appetite. It can never be filled. Everything is fleeting, even you. It can become so easy to be enticed by the things this world has to offer because that is all you see. Lust will have you compromising your values and operating outside of the will of God. Your primary goal shifts from pleasing God to pleasing yourself. But when you focus your attention toward pleasing God, you will always be satisfied.

Lust does not just surface out of the blue. There are many actions and emotions that precede lust.

Lust happens when you spend too much time and energy immersed in wrong thinking and wading in the waters of temptation. This is extremely dangerous. Part of the danger is you feel like you have everything under control, but you are unaware of the undercurrent brewing, ready to sweep you off your feet and carry you out into the deep. While you think you may have everything under control you will soon find out how out of control things really are. By then, it's too late to reign things in.

Now, even though nothing is too hard for God, you can make things hard on yourself. It may be hard to see how Christ can give you everything, especially when you can't actually see Him. This is why faith is so important. You must trust that He will provide for you. Matthew 6:33 says, "But seek first the kingdom of God and his righteousness..." and Christ will provide for your needs, whatever they may be (CSB).

Prayer:

Heavenly Father, I am struggling, and so I come to You seeking Your help. I am having feelings that I don't know how to handle, but I know You have a solution to my problem. Lord, cleanse my mind, my body, and my soul of all lustful desires. Fill me with Your Spirit. I pray with expectation and in alignment with Your will and in Your Son Jesus's name, Amen.

Reflections:

_____

_____

_____

_____

_____

MISUNDERSTOOD

*"wrongly or imperfectly understood;
not sympathetically appreciated"*[24]

24 Ibid., s.v. "misunderstood," accessed December 16, 2020,
https://www.merriam-webster.com/dictionary/misunderstood.

When people don't take the time to get to know you but instead formulate opinions of you, it can be difficult dealing with that. All we want in life is to be valued and loved. To value or love anyone, you have to take time to learn about the person. The more knowledge and insight you have about a person, the more sensitive you become to them. But we live in a society where no one wants to make time to get to know anyone. We may also find ourselves closed off from others from past hurts. So we formulate opinions about others through the narrow lens of our own experiences.

Granted, some misunderstandings may not bother you as much as others. But the problem comes in when there's a string of misunderstandings. Then one day, something that doesn't seem like such a big deal is blown out of proportion. Feeling misunderstood can sometimes make you feel sad, lonely, and isolated. This is exactly where the enemy wants you. He wants you to focus on these emotions because he knows it will only be a matter of time before you seek out unhealthy and ungodly things to make you feel better. Once you start down that road, your journey becomes inherently more difficult.

Keep in mind, you don't know yourself as well as you may think you do. So the likelihood of others knowing you fully will never happen. When others misunderstand you, ask God to help you use this as an opportunity to extend grace and mercy.

One of the things is to remember that Christ understands everything. "Our Lord is great, vast in power; his understanding is infinite" (Psalms 147:5, CSB). Remember, while He was here on earth, He, too, was misunderstood. That's sometimes hard to accept because we look to each other to really understand ourselves. We look to man to comfort us. Any time we look to anyone else other than God, we will end up feeling isolated, alone, and lonely. The Word talks about putting your faith in Jesus and not in anyone else. This doesn't mean we can't seek wise counsel on how to deal with feeling misunderstood; it just means we should not expect man to be as understanding as God.

Prayer:

Heavenly Father, it feels like I am misunderstood all the time. Lord, give me a merciful heart. When I feel misunderstood, help me to accept this as an opportunity to extend grace and forgiveness. I can come to You because you know exactly how I feel, and I know You will walk with me on this journey. I pray with expectation and in alignment with Your will and in Your Son Jesus's name, Amen.

Reflections:

_____

_____

_____

_____

_____

NUMB

"unable to think, feel, or react…"[25]

25 Ibid., s.v. "numb," accessed December 16, 2020, https://www.
merriam-webster.com/dictionary/numb.

When you are numb, it is an indication that you are so desensitized and disconnected from your situation or others that nothing affects you. This is dangerous because it blocks you from giving and receiving love.

Feeling numb is a defense mechanism resulting from being hurt over and over again. While it may seem to be a protective shield at first, numbness leads you down the path of lifelessness. Lifelessness is far from what Jesus wants us to experience. He tells us in John 10:10b, "… I have come so that they may have life and have it in abundance" (CSB).

Just like high blood pressure, numbness is a silent killer. It not only kills relationships, it kills you mentally, emotionally and spiritually. Numbness is a trick of the enemy. When you are in a place where nothing bothers you, where you're unmoved, unaffected, disconnected, detached almost to the point where you really don't care, the enemy has a greater opportunity to deceive you and win you over with his deceptive ways. He will come in and begin to nurture your wounds in a way that will have you thinking he is the only who truly cares. Once he wins your allegiance mentally and emotionally, you will begin to feel indebted to him and live a life in repayment back to him.

Remember, the Word of God says, "Therefore, with your minds ready for action, be sober-minded and set your hope completely on the grace to be brought to you at the revelation of Jesus Christ" (1 Peter 1:13, CSB). If the enemy can get you to a place where you feel numb, he has more of an opportunity to weaken you. You will not be ready and able to fight this spiritual battle effectively.

Numbness also allows for disconnection and discontent. Numbness sticks a wedge between you and others. More importantly, it sticks a wedge between you and God. When you are numb, you are empty of the desire to carry out God's mission. God came to restore us back to Him. But to do that, our hearts and minds must be open to receiving His love offering and to giving ourselves as an offering, holy and acceptable to Him (Romans 12:1, NKJV). "For if there is first a willing mind, it is accepted according to what one has, and not according to what he does not have" (2 Corinthians 8:12, NKJV). Restoration brings love, hope, joy, and peace.

Most people don't want to feel pain, so they assume it's better not to feel at all. Numbness can become a very familiar and comfortable place, but that comfort is only a smoke screen. When you allow unhealthy, impure, and ungodly thoughts into your mind and engage in ungodly activity, this allows the enemy room to creep in with hurt, anger, disappointment and depression and turn off the emotional switch. In order to defeat the enemy in this area, God says, "Above all else, guard your heart, for everything you do flows from it" (Proverbs 4:23, NIV).

Prayer:

Heavenly Father, I have been feeling numb for quite some time. This has caused me to feel disconnected from others and from You. Please restore peace, love, and hope in my life. Strengthen my heart and my mind. Restore my desire to be connected to You again. I pray with expectation and in alignment with Your will and in Your Son Jesus's name, Amen.

Reflections:

_____

_____

_____

_____

_____

OVERWHELMED

"completely overcome or overpowered by thought or feeling"[26]

---

26 Ibid., s.v. "overwhelmed," accessed December 16, 2020, https://www.merriam-webster.com/dictionary/overwhelmed.

Life has a way of bogging us down. There is always something to do, somewhere to be, or someone to cater to. How many hats are you wearing? Parent, spouse, teacher, entrepreneur, student, friend, counselor, sibling, minister… With all the responsibilities attached to each hat, it is easy to see how you can become overwhelmed. There are also times you may feel overwhelmed because you created your own chaos. You put too much on your plate, setting goals without consulting God. Are you asking God to give you peace over something that is not in His will for your life? You have to ask yourself, *did I create plans without consulting God first?* You must take a careful look in the mirror and take responsibility for your behavior.

You must learn to implement self-care. Implementing self-care doesn't mean you are being selfish. It simply means that you realize you cannot pour from an empty cup and sometimes you need a moment to refresh and rejuvenate. Within that self-care, you must be sure to spend time with God. This is not a suggestion; it is mandatory if you are ever going to find a sense of peace and balance in your life.

You will always be overwhelmed when God is not your foundation and your source. Of course, it is helpful to create to-do lists, improve your health and wellness, get massages, and rest. There is absolutely nothing wrong with having order in your life. But have you ever noticed that there are times when you do this but you still feel overwhelmed? That is because all those things are resources you can tap into, they are not the ultimate source. The truth of the matter is, if God is not first, everything is still out of order. God is the ultimate source. "The LORD gives his people strength; the LORD blesses his people with peace" (Psalm 29:11, CSB).

Prayer:

Heavenly Father, I feel overwhelmed. I don't know how I am going to accomplish all that I have to do. Please bring me peace so I can hear Your voice guide me in handling all my responsibilities. You are my refuge and strength, always ready to help me in times of trouble. I pray with expectation and in alignment with Your will and in Your Son Jesus's name, Amen.

Reflections:

_____

_____

_____

_____

_____

PRIDE

"inordinate self-esteem"[27]

---

27 Ibid., s.v. "pride," accessed December 16, 2020, https://www.merriam-webster.com/dictionary/pride.

There are various definitions associated with the word "pride." This discussion does not focus on the deep sense of pleasure of satisfaction when you achieve something. This is about having an excessively high opinion of yourself and your self-importance.

You are probably thinking, *Well, if I don't think highly of myself, then who will?* Here's the deal. God says, "Pride comes before destruction, and an arrogant spirit before a fall" (Proverbs 16:18, CSB). The reason this happens is because, when you're prideful, you have determined that you always know what is best. You are always right and you don't need to listen to anyone else. You deem yourself better than anyone else. And believe it or not, you will have a hard time obeying God.

Pride can rear its ugly head in numerous ways. Pride attaches itself to different emotions. When you look at someone who is prideful, you usually think of someone who's obvious with their arrogance. Pride is also attached to those who are judgmental. You turn your nose down at other people more often when you have an excessively high opinion of yourself.

Pride can display itself in anger. When you get angry to the point that you refuse to even listen to someone or express compassion for another person, you are prideful. You have deemed yourself lord in that situation.

It also shows up in vanity. Vanity goes beyond looking in the mirror and acknowledging your outfit is nice and your hair looks good. Vanity is when your ego and level of self-importance have been heightened to the point of worship. You worship yourself and may even secretly desire to be put on a pedestal.

Men and women are reminded in the Word of God, "...I tell everyone among you not to think of himself more highly than he should think..." (Romans 12:3a, CSB). God warns us of this because being prideful is a slippery slope that leads to destruction.

There is nothing about pride that reflects the character of Jesus Christ. Pride is a thirst that cannot be quenched. It causes you to not just want something, but to want more than everyone else has. It causes you to give to others, not because you truly want to help, but because you have a desire to feel superior. Pride will cause hate to rise in your heart because you can't stand to see others succeed.

But here is the good news. Pride can be eradicated. All you have to do is sit down and be honest about the lies you have been feeding yourself and the lies Satan has been feeding you. Seek God and ask Him to tear down the walls of pride. Commit to learning God's ways and receive His love, and watch the walls of pride come tumbling down.

Prayer:

Heavenly Father, I ask that You search me, God. You know my heart and my inner thoughts (Psalm 139:1, 23, NIV). Where there is pride, replace it with Your love and humility. I want to live a life that is pleasing to You. I pray with expectation and in alignment with Your will and in Your Son Jesus's name, Amen.

Reflections:

_____

_____

_____

_____

_____

PURPOSE

*"something set up as...the end
to be attained"*[28]

28 Ibid., s.v. "purpose," accessed December 16, 2020, https://
www.merriam-webster.com/dictionary/purpose.

Have you ever wondered why you were born? Why you are on this earth? What your purpose is? So many people go through life trying to find their purpose. They are trying to find the meaning of their existence.

They seek out palm readers, they go to school, they read books, they do any and everything possible to seek answers to this question. It is a question everyone has asked themselves at one point or another.

If you want to know the answer, I say, go to the manufacturer. Go to the One who created you. You don't go to the shoe store to get information and details about your vehicle. The car manufacturer has all the answers you need because he created the vehicle. So why do you go to counselors, philosophers, and palm readers to ask them about the purpose of your existence? The Bible tells us, "… we are his workmanship, created in Christ Jesus for good works, which God prepared ahead of time for us to do" (Ephesians 2:10, CSB). There is your answer. We were created in Christ Jesus for good works; meaning we were created to live holy lives and follow His Word. As we do this, He will work in our lives in such a way that gives us more insight on how He will use us in our families and our careers.

Here is the thing, though. Walking in your purpose is not always easy. You can never truly operate in your purpose if you don't have faith. The

Word tells us, "…Without faith it is impossible to please God…" (Hebrews 11:6a, CSB). Faith is not just saying that you know; it's walking like you know. This means there are plenty of times you have to act based on God's Word. You need to operate in a way that says "I see it" even before you see it. Walking by faith is all about having a true experience with God.

Prayer:

Heavenly Father, there have been times I questioned my purpose here on earth. I ask that You remove anything from my life that hinders me from fully embracing your purpose for my life. Equip me with everything I need to fulfill the plan and purpose for my life. I pray with expectation and in alignment with Your will and in Your Son Jesus's name, Amen.

Reflections:

_____

_____

_____

_____

_____

REJECTION

*"the act of not accepting, believing,
or considering something..."*[29]

---

29 Ibid., s.v. "rejection," accessed December 16, 2020, https://
www.merriam-webster.com/dictionary/rejection.

How many times have you felt like you were not good enough? How many times have people told you they love you, but didn't choose you? How many interviews have you been on only for every employer to say "no?"

If you get rejected often enough, you are likely to start developing feelings of low self-esteem. You begin to feel like you are worthless. Loneliness and depression may even creep in. You shut down and isolate. Rejection is a dangerous emotion to settle into. Rejection will have you connecting with the wrong people and running in wrong crowds just to fit in. You will slip into a reckless lifestyle. You may feel that just because you may not be using drugs or robbing a bank, life has not become reckless. But anything you do that compromises your relationship with God is reckless.

This is exactly where the enemy wants you. He wants you to question everything, even the God you serve. He wants to get you to a place where life seems like one big ball of rejection and if God, the giver of life, put you here, well then, He must have also rejected you. You feel like God is not answering your prayers or delivering you from your trials. So God's plan must be flawed. But once again, this is far from the truth.

From the beginning of time Satan has been a formidable foe. His job is to cast doubt into your mind and have you believe no one cares about you. But God's word is true. "...the LORD will not reject his people; he will never forsake his inheritance" (Psalms 94:14, NIV). So much of this battle is fought in the mind. We must immerse ourselves in the Word because when it is time to fight, our minds have to be strong.

You are not forgotten, nor have you been rejected. You have been chosen as a Kingdom Soldier. Any rejection you may experience is simply to strengthen you, an opportunity for God to use that pain to mold you into His image; to prepare you for future battles to come; to help someone else. There is nothing wrong with you. The enemy is just doing his job. But God's got you!

Prayer:

Heavenly Father, there are times when I feel like the entire world is against me. I admit that some-times I want to belong in this world so badly that I forget you made me to stand out in You and not fit in (Romans 12:2). I see now that every door You closed was only for my protection. Thank You for embracing me and welcoming me into Your Kingdom. I pray with expectation and in alignment with Your will and in Your Son Jesus's name, Amen.

Reflections:

_____

_____

_____

_____

_____

RESENTMENT

"a feeling of indignant displeasure or persistent ill will at something regarded as a wrong, insult, or injury"[30]

---

30 Ibid., s.v. "resentment," accessed December 16, 2020, https://www.merriam-webster.com/dictionary/resentment.

Resentment is a level of anger, annoyance, and displeasure that goes to the point of becoming bitter. It is a deep level of anger that has caused you to wish ill, sometimes going so far as to carry out that ill-will. Resentment is not a surface-layer emotion. By the time you start feeling resentful toward someone or something, it has gone beyond the surface and embedded itself in your heart. This is such a dangerous place to be. You never want anything other than God's character to be embedded in you.

Resentment is like a cancer that eats away at you. When you hold on to resentment too long, it opens the door for you to feel anger or negative feelings towards yourself for even allowing yourself to be stuck in your situation. Emotions like misery and rage are not far behind. This is a recipe for disaster.

Dealing with resentment is a matter that requires God's special touch. Resentment finds its way into your heart through unresolved hurt, anger, and unforgiveness. You've got to learn how to forgive and deal with your anger early. These emotions tempt you to resort to acts that put your soul in danger. The Word warns us now to "...put away all the following anger, wrath, malice, slander, and filthy language from your mouth" (Colossians 3:8, CSB) These things only lead us to engage in acts of unrighteousness and sin. Sin kills your mind, your body, and your soul. Today, ask the Lord to help you develop a righteous indignation against sin and stand so firm on His Word of God, as it is really the only thing that can tear down the walls of resentment.

Prayer:

Heavenly Father, I need Your help. Please remove my resentment and release any anger I may be holding on to. Resentment only turns my thoughts away from You and leads me astray. Whenever someone offends me, help me to practice for- giveness. Instead of resentment, let seeds of love and reconciliation grow in my heart. I pray with expectation and in alignment with Your will and in Your Son Jesus's name, Amen.

Reflections:

_____

_____

_____

_____

_____

SADNESS

"affected with or expressive of grief or unhappiness"[31]

---

31 Ibid., s.v. "sadness," accessed December 16, 2020, https://www.merriam-webster.com/dictionary/sadness.

Showing sadness is not a sign of weakness. It is a sign of humanness. There is nothing abnormal about sadness. Even Jesus expressed sadness a couple of times during His ministry here on earth. When you experience loss, you may feel somewhat emotional and sad. When injustice and devastation seem to surround you, sometimes sadness and heaviness can descend on you.

However, allow me to caution you. If not addressed, sadness can easily morph into depression. Have you ever heard the saying: "Bad news travels fast"? It works the same way when it comes to emotions. It doesn't take long for sadness to transform into depression, despair, misery, gloom, and suicidal thoughts. Once they join the party, it's hard to get them to leave. You may even feel like you're forced to wear a happy face, and that's an additional burden.

Sometimes sadness manifests itself in the form of physical pain. Whether we want to believe it or not, everything is intertwined. Emotions are not bad, we just have to be careful not to allow our emotions to dictate our decisions. Operating in your emotions will cause you to act in desperation. You may find yourself doing anything to remove the pain. Addictions and destructive relationships form as a result of trying to dull the pain.

No one likes to be in pain. No one likes sadness. So when most people feel sad, they attempt to fill the void themselves. Well, that's the problem. Christ has to fill the void. He is the One who redeems you. "The LORD is near the brokenhearted; he saves those crushed in spirit" (Psalm 34:18, CSB). Sometimes the weight of your sadness can blind you and cause you to forget that Christ is there for you. He is willing to deliver you from the weight of your sorrow. When your heart is broken and your spirit is crushed, God is standing by, ready to help you put the pieces back together again.

Prayer:

Heavenly Father, my heart is heavy. You are the Prince of Peace. I ask that You would remove this sadness and replace it with peace and joy. Help me to remember that when I place my hope in You, I will find peace. I pray with expectation and in alignment with Your will and in Your Son Jesus's name, Amen.

Reflections:

_____

_____

_____

_____

_____

SHAME

*"a painful emotion caused by consciousness of guilt,
shortcoming, or impropriety"*[32]

---

32 Ibid., s.v. "shame," accessed December 16, 2020, https://www.
merriam-webster.com/dictionary/shame.

Have you ever done something you know you should not have done and someone else found out? Have you ever felt humiliated about what you have done, thinking everyone knows even when no one really knows. Shame makes you want to hide in a dark corner and isolate yourself from others. Shame affects your confidence. It can make you feel like you are down in the gutter. You may feel like you are always second-guessing yourself.

Insecurities begin to surface. It feels like no matter how good anyone says you are, feelings of worthlessness and loneliness loom in the shadows. And believe it or not, it can have you flow right back into the same behavior which caused these feelings to begin with.

Shame will cause you to be dishonest. If you can't be honest, you will never be able to reach the core of your problem. And if you can't get to the core of your problem, you can never truly be healed.

The embarrassment you feel may cause you to shut down and not reach out for help. And I get it. It is hard to find somebody with whom you can be transparent; someone who can hold your pain without condemnation. This is why I love God. He tells us, "...there is now no condemnation for those in Christ Jesus, because the law of the Spirit of life in Christ Jesus has set you free from the law of sin and death" (Romans 8:1-2, CSB). That doesn't mean that He doesn't correct us. It means He doesn't throw us away or say that we are unsalvageable. He does not sentence us to death. He offers grace, mercy, and forgiveness and restores you back to Him. Remember that as you move forward.

Prayer:

Heavenly Father, I have repented, and I choose to receive the gift of Your Son, Jesus Christ. Because I have accepted Jesus Christ, I believe and declare that there is therefore now no condemnation for me! You have released me from my shame. I pray with expectation and in alignment with Your will and in Your Son Jesus's name, Amen.

Reflections:

_____

_____

_____

_____

_____

SUICIDAL

"dangerous especially to life... being or performing a deliberate act resulting in the voluntary death of the person who does it"[33]

33 Ibid., s.v. "suicidal," accessed December 16, 2020, https://www.merriam-webster.com/dictionary/suicidal.

Life will present challenges that bring you to your highest level of vulnerability.

When you are suicidal, you feel as though there is absolutely no solution in sight that will resolve your problem and ease your pain. You are blinded by guilt, shame, depression, loneliness, anxiety, anger, betrayal, isolation, and rejection. They have all become too overwhelming for you to bear.

It's not that you want life to end, you just want the pain to end. You have become mentally, emotionally, physically, and spiritually tired. If others could see the internal scars and the wounds you have accumulated, they would see you are in a coma on life support. You feel emotionally and spiritually dead, with the grace of God being the only thing keeping your heart beating.

The embarrassment you may feel from being suicidal will cause you to shut down and not reach out for help. And I get it. It is hard to find somebody who can hold your pain without condemnation. But rest assured God has someone He can use to speak a word to you, a word that will resurrect life within you again. He would be unjust God to allow His people to be here on earth and not provide avenues for them to be built up, revived, and rejuvenated. If you are thinking of ending your own life, please call your local suicide hotline. God can speak hope to you through the counselors on the other end.

The only way to get through is to put *all* your trust and hope in Jesus. When we do this, He promises to give us what we need. He tells us in His Word, "…may the God of hope fill you with all joy and peace as you believe so that you may overflow with hope by the power of the Holy Spirit" (Romans 15:13, CSB).

Sometimes the only thing that keeps you holding on is the child you don't want to leave behind or the family member who would be so distraught. But God wants you to know He has a greater purpose for you. Just like a child, trust that, while you may not see or understand everything your parent does, God's purpose is never to bring you harm. It is to help you get to a glorious end.

You may not see how things will work out, but God sees the way, as He is the Way (John 14:6). Don't try to figure it out. Treat God the way you treat Advil when you have a headache. You don't call the manufacturer and bombard him with questions on how all the ingredients within the little pill are going to work together to stop your headache. You trust that the maker knows what he is doing, and you pop that pill with the expectation that your headache will subside.

There is hope. Follow God. Trust His plan and I guarantee you everything will work out.

Prayer:

Heavenly Father, I give you permission to enter my life to remove suicidal thoughts from my mind. Help me to see that there is hope and a future in You. You said in your word I am an overcomer and that's what I believe. Suicidal thoughts will no longer overtake me. I pray with expectation and in alignment with Your will and in Your Son Jesus's name, Amen.

Reflections:

_____

_____

_____

_____

_____

TIRED

"drained of strength and energy;
fatigued often to the point of exhaustion;
worn out by hard use"[34]

---

34 Ibid., s.v. "tired," accessed December 16, 2020, https://www.merriam-webster.com/dictionary/tired.

When your mind can't rest, nothing can rest. Have you ever been so stressed that you slept all night long without interruption and still woke up exhausted? You can become so mentally drained that fatigue and exhaustion will affect your physical body as well. So what can you do? Experts tell you to avoid eating certain foods, turn the TV off before you go to sleep, get more exercise, get a massage, and meditate, just to name a few. While I am all for providing practical tools on how to manage fatigue more effectively, I find that most experts tend to leave out one main ingredient: God.

God tells us in Jeremiah 31:25, "...I [fully] satisfy the weary soul, and I replenish every languishing *and* sorrowful person" (AMP). God promises rest to everyone who comes to Him; rest for your soul, mind, and emotions. If we don't go to Christ, we will always be tired, discouraged, stressed, and depressed.

One major problem is we keep using God as a resource. God keeps telling us, "I'm not just a tool you can put in your toolkit. I am The Source." If you go to Him, He will give you everything you need. Yes, you need to get sleep. Yes, you need to eat correctly. Yes, you need to exercise. I'm not taking any of those things away. I am simply saying those things are meaningless if the foundation is not in place. Look at it this way. The frame to a home is useless if the foundation to the home has not been laid correctly. This journey is not intended for you to walk alone. You will never be able to bear the weight of the world. That is why Christ came. Allow Christ to do what He came to do.

Prayer:

Heavenly Father, I am tired and overwhelmed. The constant struggles and demands feel intense some days. It's just hard to keep going in the face of defeat and discouragement. Forgive me for the times I have failed to allow You to work in me so I may receive Your strength. Help me to keep my eyes on You. I will look to the hills from whence cometh my help, and I know my help is in You (Psalm 121:1, KJV). I pray with expectation and in alignment with Your will and in Your Son Jesus's name, Amen.

Reflections:

_____

_____

_____

_____

_____

THREATENED

*"having an uncertain chance of
continued survival"*[35]

---

35 Ibid., s.v. "threatened," accessed December 16, 2020, https://
www.merriam-webster.com/dictionary/threatened.

The enemy's greatest weapons are fear and intimidation. And he uses those weapons every chance he gets to instill fear into the hearts and mind of people. He replays tapes in your mind of old experiences that weren't so great. He does this by negative talk from yourself or others. Once fear is instilled in your heart, you become quite easy to intimidate, and thus easily threatened.

The enemy's plan is to intentionally harm you and take hostile action toward you. Jesus cautions us in John 10:10, "The thief comes only to steal and kill and destroy; I have come that they may have life, and have it to the full" (NIV). Satan is a thief, determined to take hostile action against you. Satan is on a mission to thwart God's plan, and he will do anything and use anybody to do it. The enemy knows how to do his job well. However, Jesus came to do a job, also, and that is to give life. The question comes down to this, *who will you believe?*

You see, to believe means more than just knowing something is true. It means to be sure, certain, strong, and unwavering in what you say you know. So when the enemy threatens you and launches his attacks, will you believe him and be afraid? Or will you stand firm on the Word of God, which says "Be strong and of good courage, do not fear nor be afraid of them; for the LORD your God, He *is* the One who goes with you. He will not leave you nor forsake you" (Deuteronomy 31:6, NKJV).

God protects his own. While the enemy may plot to harm you and stop you from experiencing the fullness of God, God has a plan designed to deliver you from the enemy's hand.

Prayer:

Heavenly Father, I pray that You would protect me and cast down every threat the enemy throws my way. I know You are all powerful, and I stand on Your Word. Your love surrounds me daily, so I will not fear when the enemy comes against me. My trust is in You, Lord. I pray with expectation and in alignment with Your will and in Your Son Jesus's name, Amen.

Reflections:

_____

_____

_____

_____

_____

TRAPPED

*"a position or situation from which
it is difficult or impossible to escape"*[36]

36 Ibid., s.v. "trapped," accessed December 16, 2020, https://
www.merriam-webster.com/dictionary/trapped.

There are many situations people are involved in where they feel trapped. It could be a horrible job. It could be a bad marriage. You can be trapped in any situation. It could be a decision that changed the trajectory of your life. Sometimes we're trapped in situations because of our own doing. Everything is not always someone else's fault.

But don't worry, as always, here comes God to the rescue! "He brought me up from a desolate pit: out of the muddy clay, and set my feet on a rock, making my steps secure" (Psalm 40:2, CSB). He always makes a way of escape. He knows this world is corrupt. He would be an unjust God if he did not offer His people protection along with an escape plan.

Jesus came so we could have life and we could have it more abundantly. He came to give us what this world could never give us. Think about it, no good parent is going to just sit there and allow their child to suffer. They will offer options, resources, comfort, and support. God does the same. He always provides answers that lead to life (John 14:6).

Remember, feeling trapped does not have to be a permanent state of being. God offers solutions. However, His solutions come with conditions. Oftentimes, many people think of God like a genie. All they have to do is close their eyes and make a wish and like magic all your desires are fulfilled. That is not the case. God's love is precious, and He will not allow anyone to manipulate His love. Jesus clearly says "…If you keep my commands you will remain in my love…" (John 15:10a, CSB). The only way you will reap the benefits of freedom is *if* you obey His voice and follow His commandments. Just like in real life, the only way you will be exempt from getting a speeding ticket is if you obey the law and observe the speed limit posted on the highway.

Prayer:

Heavenly Father, I feel trapped in my current situation. Give me eyes to see where You are leading me, ears to hear Your instructions, and the courage and will to follow Your commands. I know You have plans to give me hope and a future. Please surround me with Your grace and mercy as I walk confidently in Your ways. I pray with expectation and in alignment with Your will and in Your Son Jesus's name, Amen.

Reflections:

_____

_____

_____

_____

_____

UNFORGIVING

"having or making no allowance for error or weakness"[37]

---

37   Ibid., s.v. "unforgiving," accessed December 16, 2020, https://
www.merriam-webster.com/dictionary/unforgiving.

Forgiveness is one of the core teachings of Christ, yet many struggle with embracing it. Unforgiveness is a portal the enemy uses so he can rest in your heart, settle in your mind, and rule your life. Unforgiveness affects every fiber of your being; mentally, emotionally, physically, and spiritually.

Why is it so hard to forgive? Pride is one of many reasons people find it difficult to forgive. Pride is a preference for your will over God's will. When you are offended, most likely the human side of you wants to enact revenge and see the offender suffer. But God's will is that none should be lost and "that all come to repentance" (2 Peter 3:9, NKJV).

When emotions are running high and you are caught up in your feelings, forgiveness is a difficult pill to swallow. That's not to say that you haven't been violated or betrayed in horrific ways. However, when you operate with the love of Christ, forgiveness becomes more easily digestible. Forgiveness doesn't mean there are not consequences for the offender's actions. Forgiveness says you have made a conscious decision to allow God to avenge your case. You allow God to deal with the other person's heart in a way that only He can.

Whenever possible, have a conversation with the person who offended you. God clearly tells us, "If your brother sins against you, go tell him his fault, between you and him alone. If he listens to you, you have won your brother." (Matthew 18:15, CSB). One of the reasons He tells you to have a conversation with your brother is because keeping the issue bottled up allows it to fester in your mind, heart, and spirit. When issues fester, they breed anger, bitterness, and resentment, which inherently lead to vengeful acts. Everything you do comes from a place of punishment, not reconciliation or redemption.

Forgiveness doesn't mean you walk around with someone who offended you acting like nothing happened. It doesn't mean you don't feel hurt, disappointed, or betrayed. It means that you recognize the need to turn your hurts over to God, knowing that He is the only one who can heal your broken heart and work on the heart of the offender so you might be restored back to each other. Forgiveness releases you from the self-inflicted responsibility to change a person, and it releases the offender from the guilt of the offense as that person becomes remorseful, turns to God for forgiveness, and changes his ways. Now, both of you can live in the freedom of Jesus Christ.

Prayer:

Heavenly Father, thank You for Your gift of forgiveness. There is a healing power in forgiveness that only You can provide. Teach me how to extend forgiveness to others just as You have extended grace and forgiveness to me. Help me walk in Your righteousness and peace demonstrating

Your love here on earth. I pray with expectation and in alignment with Your will and in Your Son Jesus's name, Amen.

Reflections:

_____

_____

_____

_____

_____

UNSURE OF HEARING GOD'S VOICE

Have you ever been unsure if you heard God's voice? Sometimes you really ask yourself this question when you follow through on what you thought was His directive, only to find out that you might have been wrong.

This is a sensitive topic, because the truth is, sometimes your personal desire for something can be so great that it can be difficult to discern whether something is part of God's will or your will. To discern the voice of God, you must be diligent about seeking Him daily. You must be intentional about developing a relationship with Him. This is how you get to know Him. When you do this, He will speak concerning various matters in your life. And because you have been seeking Him, you will be able to hear Him and follow Him. "My sheep hear my voice, I know them, and they follow me" (John 10:27, CSB). Some of the blockage comes when you are disconnected.

The reason we can't hear Him sometimes is because we are not still and quiet enough to listen. Hearing from God comes through prayer, meditation, and reading His Word. He will always reveal to you what you need to know.

One of the toughest things about hearing God's voice is the waiting period. Sometimes He doesn't answer right away, and the silence produces stress and anxiety. Don't allow fear to cause you to operate outside God's will. If you are waiting for an answer, but you are in a position where you must make a decision, do your best to decide in accordance with God's Word. I guarantee you will not go wrong. If it ends up being the right decision, wonderful. If not, don't worry. He will use it for your good and for His glory. I am a firm believer that, even if you don't know exactly what to do, the Holy Spirit living inside you will prompt you when there is something you definitely should not do. He will lead and direct you accordingly. With Jesus as your guide, you can't go wrong

How do the answers come? They may come in a scripture, a dream, a word from God through someone, or a supernatural calm. God knows how to speak to each one of His children in a way where He knows the message will come through. He did it for Elijah when He spoke to him in a still small voice. "Then He said, 'Go out, and stand on the mountain before the LORD.' And behold, the LORD passed by, and a great and strong wind tore into the mountains and broke the rocks in pieces before the LORD, *but* the LORD *was* not in the wind; and after the wind an earthquake, *but* the LORD *was* not in the earthquake; and after the earthquake a fire, *but* the LORD *was* not in the fire; and after the fire a still small voice"(1 Kings 19: 11-12, NKJV). Sometimes, we wait for the thunder to roll and the lightning to flash, but God doesn't need to yell to get His point across.

Prayer:

Heavenly Father, I have a lot of decisions to make. I come to you today seeking Your will. Help me to know Your voice and not be deceived by other voices. I need Your instruction and guidance. Help me confirm Your voice through Your Word. I pray with expectation and in alignment with Your will and in Your Son Jesus's name, Amen.

Reflections:

_____

_____

_____

_____

_____

VINDICTIVE

"disposed to seek revenge"[38]

---

38 Ibid., s.v. "vindictive," accessed December 16, 2020, https://www.merriam-webster.com/dictionary/vindictive.

It's easy for someone with lingering anger to eventually want to take revenge. Being eager to harm someone is not the type of spirit you should possess. This eagerness doesn't always present itself in the form excitement like you are on your way to an amusement park. Sometimes it is a strong, focused urge where you are so fixated on a particular outcome that you will take any means necessary to get the results you want. When you get to this point, there is now an open portal for greed and revenge to enter. Your appetite for retribution has now entered the danger zone. This puts you in the mindset of feeling like you are more powerful than you really are. You start conjuring up evil thoughts on what you can do to get someone back.

The Bible says if you become angry, don't sin. "Be angry and do not sin. Don't let the sun go down on your anger, and don't give the devil an opportunity" (Ephesians 4:26-27, CSB). The devil is waiting for any opportunity to move you out of the will of God. When anger is not managed appropriately, it will turn into bitterness, which will lead to a vindictive spirit. Once you get into that mindset, you will unknowingly digging a ditch for yourself, as well.

Remember God takes care of His own. When someone has offended you, God says, "Do not take revenge, my dear friends, but leave room for God's wrath, for it is written: 'It is mine to avenge; I will repay,' says the Lord" (Romans 12:19, NIV). God does not take revenge, but He will enact righteous judgment in the interest of justice. To take revenge is to operate in bitterness with the goal to harm another for a wrong they committed. God is about restoration. God wants to bring us back to Him under peace and love. So how can a God that's all about restoration harbor bitterness? When God says, "It is mine to avenge," He is simply saying He will make the wrong right.

God will usher in perfect justice for His people. No man can restore all that has been taken from you. God doesn't operate like man, where He seeks an eye for an eye. He promises true and complete restoration for everything that you lost. Rest easy knowing that God will settle your account.

Prayer:

Heavenly Father, I want to operate with Your love and Your wisdom. Remove all bitterness from my heart. Give me the strength to treat even my worst enemies with love and mercy, knowing that You are the only One who can enact righteous judgment and ensure that everything I lost is restored completely. I pray with expectation and in alignment with Your will and in Your Son Jesus's name, Amen.

Reflections:

_____

_____

_____

_____

_____

WEAK

"lacking strength…"[39]

---

39 Ibid., s.v. "weak," accessed December 16, 2020, https://www.merriam-webster.com/dictionary/weak.

Have you ever felt like you were too weak to walk away from something, or too weak to stay where you are? It takes strength to stand up for the right thing and walk away from the wrong thing.

The problem is sometimes people try to do things in their own strength. They try to exercise their willpower. Well, if willpower always worked, then you wouldn't need God. You need more than strong self-determination to prevent yourself from falling prey to the attacks of the enemy. If all you needed was your self-determination, that would mean Jesus died and rose from the grave in vain. That would mean He lied when He said, "All authority has been given to Me in heaven and on earth" (Matthew 28:18, NKJV). Since we know His death was not in vain and that God is not a liar, we can conclude that in order for us to defeat the enemy, we must be connected to the One with all power. Satan doesn't fear you. He fears the God in you and that is Who he bows down to.

Stop allowing your ego and pride to trick you into thinking you don't need God. Pride and ego are deceptive and inflate your senses of power and control. God clearly tells us in His word to "Look to the LORD and his strength; seek his face always" (1 Chronicles 16:11, NIV). You cannot fight the enemy in your own strength. You cannot be an overcomer and win spiritual battles in your own flesh. You must see God and rely on His strength if you are going to defeat the enemy. He is the One who defeats depression, anxiety, suicidal thoughts, jealousy, loneliness, and shame. He is the One who gives you the courage and strength to follow His commands.

When you feel weak. just know that you can do all things through Christ who strengthens you (Philippians 4:13, NKJV). You no longer need to bear the burden of strengthening yourself when you feel weak. God's got you.

Prayer:

Heavenly Father, whenever I am faced with a challenge that makes me feel weak, remind me that is it not by my strength or by my might, but by Your Spirit that I am able to defeat the enemy (Zechariah 4:6, NKJV). I pray with expectation and in alignment with Your will and in Your Son Jesus's name, Amen.

Reflections:

_____

_____

_____

_____

_____

WORTHLESS

"lacking worth: valueless; useless"[40]

---

40 Ibid., s.v. "worthless," accessed December 16, 2020, https://www.merriam-webster.com/dictionary/worthless.

Have you ever felt like you are just not good enough? This feeling is often fueled by social media, negative talk from others, and adults in your childhood. Society has a way of establishing definitions for what it means to be worthy. When you feel like you don't measure up, you find yourself exhausting all avenues trying to meet society's standards. It is amazing how impactful society can be. We're driven a lot by what we see, how society treats us, and what these experiences instill in us when we're young.

This only leads to self-destruction. You begin to feel like you are not capable. You label yourself as a failure, all because you couldn't measure up to a standard that another person—who's doing the same thing because they're unsatisfied with their life—put in place.

Do you find yourself overcompensating in other areas of life? What areas of life are you overcompensating in? Is your personality over the top? Do you find yourself spending more money than you should? Are you trying to obtain every degree in academia? Ask yourself, *am I trying to prove my worth to the world by doing these things?*

Constantly comparing yourself to others and trying to live up to other people's expectations is exhausting. This drains you mentally, emotionally, physically, and spiritually.

Just because you haven't reached your career goals, gotten down to your desired weight, or married the love of your life yet doesn't mean you are a failure. Your standards and goals should be based on the Word of God. If you trust Him and do your part, He is faithful to give you everything He has for you.

It does not matter what other people say. God does not think you are unworthy. You are one of His valued children. You are important in His eyes. This is how valuable you are to Him: "... God showed his love among us: He sent his one and only Son into the world that we might live through him. This is love: not that we loved God, but that he loved us and sent his Son as an atoning sacrifice for our sins" (1 John 4:9-10, CSB). I don't know anyone who would offer up their only child for anything. Only God!

Oftentimes, when we feel worthless, there are emotions lying beneath the surface. Feeling unwanted and unloved are what burdens so many people. Everyone wants to be loved. This is the very reason God sent His son; to love us with a love that runs deeper than any human can imagine.

I know you are saying, *That all sounds great, but on my best days I find my insecurities rising up to overtake me.* I am not saying it is always easy; no battle ever is. That is why it is called a "battle." To fight this battle effectively and work through feelings of worthlessness, you have to shift your perspective. When we remember to see ourselves as Christ see us, then we have the proper perspective. The only way to gain this perspective is to immerse yourself in the Word of God.

Prayer:

Heavenly Father, I am struggling. I feel like I don't matter, and I feel like I am not important. I feel so worthless. I feel like I don't measure up and I have become exhausted at the very notion of trying. Sometimes I feel like my life has no purpose. Sometimes all I seem to hear are the messages that echo in my mind constantly, reminding me that I am not good enough. I know Your Word is the only thing that speaks truth about who I am and how valuable I am to You. Help me to embrace that truth. I pray with expectation and in alignment with Your will and in Your Son Jesus's name, Amen.

Reflections:

_____

_____

_____

_____

_____

Now that you've finished reading *Matters of the Heart*, I'd love to hear what you thought of it! You can do this by writing an honest review on the Amazon listing—it will also help other readers find the best book for them. Or, you can send me an email at info@withinyourreach.life. I can't wait to hear from you!

Endnotes

1. *Merriam-Webster Dictionary*, s.v., "abused," accessed December 16, 2020, https://www.merriam-webster.com/dictionary/abused.

2. Ibid., s.v. "anger," accessed, December 16, 2020, https://www.merriam-webster.com/dictionary/anger.

3. Ibid., s.v. "anxious," accessed December 16, 2020, https://www.merriam-webster.com/dictionary/anxious.

4. Ibid., s.v. "betrayed," accessed December 16, 2020, https://www.merriam-webster.com/dictionary/betrayed.

5. Ibid., s.v. "confused," accessed December 16, 2020, https://www.merriam-webster.com/dictionary/confused.

6. Ibid., s.v. "defeated," accessed December 16, 2020, https://www.merriam-webster.com/dictionary/defeated.

7. Ibid., s.v. "depressed," accessed December 16, 2020, https://www.merriam-webster.com/dictionary/depressed.

8. Ibid., s.v. "devastated," accessed December 16, 2020, https://www.merriam-webster.com/dictionary/devastated.

9. Ibid., s.v. "disappointed," accessed December 16, 2020, https://www.merriam-webster.com/dictionary/disappointed.

10. Ibid., s.v. "distrustful," accessed December 16, 2020, https://www.merriam-webster.com/dictionary/distrustful.

11. Ibid., s.v. "fear," accessed December 16, 2020, https://www.merriam-webster.com/dictionary/fear.

12. Ibid., s.v. "forgotten," accessed December 16, 2020, https://www.merriam-webster.com/dictionary/forgotten.

13. Ibid., s.v. "guilt," accessed December 16, 2020, https://www.merriam-webster.com/dictionary/guilt.

14. Ibid., s.v. "hopeless," accessed December 16, 2020, https://www.merriam-webster.com/dictionary/hopeless.

15. Ibid., s.v., "impatient," accessed December 16, 2020, https://www.merriam-webster.com/dictionary/impatient.

16. Ibid., s.v. "indecisive," accessed December 16, 2020, https://www.merriam-webster.com/dictionary/indecisive.

17. Ibid., s.v. "insecurity," accessed December 16, 2020, https://www.merriam-webster.com/dictionary/insecurity.

18. Ibid., s.v. "isolated," accessed December 16, 2020, https://www.merriam-webster.com/dictionary/isolated.

19. Ibid., s.v. "jealousy," accessed December 16, 2020, https://www.merriam-webster.com/dictionary/jealousy.

20. "Sense of Entitlement," Out of the FOG, accessed December 7, 2020, https://outofthefog.website/top-100-trait-blog/2015/11/4/sense-of-entitlement, quoted in Robert Porter, "The Psychology Behind Sense of Entitlement," Better Help, last modified June 25, 2020.

21. *Merriam-Webster Dictionary*, s.v. "judgmental," accessed December 16, 2020, https://www.merriam-webster.com/dictionary/judgmental.

22. Ibid., s.v. "loneliness," accessed December 16, 2020, https://www.merriam-webster.com/dictionary/loneliness.

23. Ibid., s.v. "lust," accessed December 16, 2020, https://www.merriam-webster.com/dictionary/lust.

24. Ibid., s.v. "misunderstood," accessed December 16, 2020, https://www.merriam-webster.com/dictionary/misunderstood.

25. Ibid., s.v. "numb," accessed December 16, 2020, https://www.merriam-webster.com/dictionary/numb.

26. Ibid., s.v. "overwhelmed," accessed December 16, 2020, https://www.merriam-webster.com/dictionary/overwhelmed.

27. Ibid., s.v. "pride," accessed December 16, 2020, https://www.merriam-webster.com/dictionary/pride.

28. Ibid., s.v. "purpose," accessed December 16, 2020, https://www.merriam-webster.com/dictionary/purpose.

29. Ibid., s.v. "rejection," accessed December 16, 2020, https://www.merriam-webster.com/dictionary/rejection.

30. Ibid., s.v. "resentment," accessed December 16, 2020, https://www.merriam-webster.com/dictionary/resentment.

31. Ibid., s.v. "sadness," accessed December 16, 2020, https://www.merriam-webster.com/dictionary/sadness.

32. Ibid., s.v. "shame," accessed December 16, 2020, https://www.merriam-webster.com/dictionary/shame.

33. Ibid., s.v. "suicidal," accessed December 16, 2020, https://www.merriam-webster.com/dictionary/suicidal.

34. Ibid., s.v. "tired," accessed December 16, 2020, https://www.merriam-webster.com/dictionary/tired.

35. Ibid., s.v. "threatened," accessed December 16, 2020, https://www.merriam-webster.com/dictionary/threatened.

36. Ibid., s.v. "trapped," accessed December 16, 2020, https://www.merriam-webster.com/dictionary/trapped.

37. Ibid., s.v. "unforgiving," accessed December 16, 2020, https://www.merriam-webster.com/dictionary/unforgiving.

38. Ibid., s.v. "vindictive," accessed December 16, 2020, https://www.merriam-webster.com/dictionary/vindictive.

39. Ibid., s.v. "weak," accessed December 16, 2020, https://www.merriam-webster.com/dictionary/weak.

40. Ibid., s.v. "worthless," accessed December 16, 2020, https://www.merriam-webster.com/dictionary/worthless.

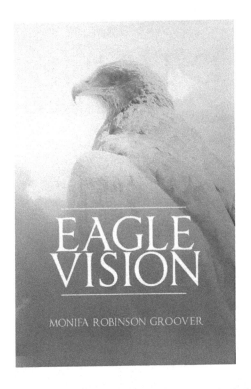

EAGLE
VISION

MONIFA ROBINSON GROOVER

Never allow your knowledge, skills, and abilities to take you where your vision, character and strength can't keep you! *Eagle Vision* moves beyond what can be taught in life (skills, knowledge, abilities) and focuses on operating with excellence daily. This is a book for those who want to excel above and beyond to reach their personal "top," by creating goals while maintaining integrity throughout the process. A parallel is drawn to the majestic eagle, whose very persona is captured to illustrate the excellence that can be attained through vision, rising above storms and intentionality.

Available worldwide at all major online retailers.

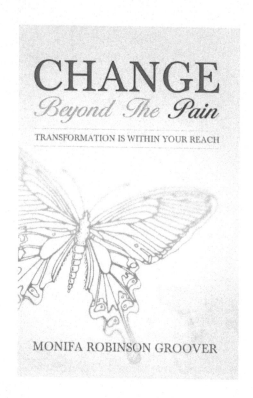

CHANGE
Beyond The Pain
TRANSFORMATION IS WITHIN YOUR REACH

MONIFA ROBINSON GROOVER

This book will teach you how to transform your life. Utilizing the strength of the Word of God and this guide as a tool *Change Beyond The Pain* will empower you to gain a deeper understanding of what God is trying to impart in all of us.

Change Beyond The Pain will help you discover:

- How true healing comes from allowing God to transform your life.

- How to stop repeating the same cycles of hurt, anger, fear and depression.

- That God has a plan for your life.

- There is power and purpose in your pain to help you experience positive and productive transformation.

You will learn how to move beyond accepting change to embracing transformation. So, if you are seeking restoration, read this book with and open your heart, and together with your bible let the transformation begin.

Available worldwide at all major online retailers.

This companion workbook will guide you as you
embark upon your spiritual journey. If you are
seeking restoration read this book with an open
heart and together with your Bible, let the transformation begin.

Available worldwide at all major online retailers.

About the Author

Like many, Monifa is no stranger to the roller-coaster of life. Though she encountered challenges on her journey, Monifa learned firsthand that a strong foundation in the Word of God is the only sure way to escape the grip of the enemy. She is grateful for how her experiences and faith continue to shape her into the woman God has called her to be. She is committed to sharing her lessons with others so they too can be free to live the abundant life God has destined for them. Her hope is to inspire others to live life "on purpose" and not haphazardly.

Since 2004, Monifa has worked with women in leadership roles to find balance and fulfillment in their lives through:

- Leadership Training & Professional Development
- Individual & Group Coaching Services
- Workshops/Conferences/Retreats
- Keynote Speaking

Some of her most popular teachings, classes, and conferences include: Leadership 101, Personal Growth & Development, Professional Ethics, and Eagle Vision. Discovery calls can be booked directly with Monifa and her team on her website: withinyourreach.life.

Contact Monifa today!

Within Your Reach
Email: info@withinyourreach.life
Phone: 404-836-3905

Twitter: @WYRInspires
Instagram: @WYRInspires
Facebook: @WYRConsulting
Youtube: Within Your Reach Consulting Services, LLC

Vision Publishing House, LLC
P.O. Box 60393
Savannah, GA 31420

Email: info@withinyourreach.life

Made in USA - Kendallville, IN
1223252_9780983677673
01.08.2021 1503